A Question of Class

Lindsey German

A Question of Class

Lindsey German

BOOKMARKS

London, Chicago and Sydney

A Question of Class – Lindsey German
First published July 1996
Bookmarks, 265 Seven Sisters Road, London N4 2DE, England
Bookmarks, PO Box 16085, Chicago Il. 60616, USA
Bookmarks, PO Box A338, Sydney South Australia
Copyright c Bookmarks Publications Ltd

ISBN 1 898876 05 3

Printed by Lavenham Press
Cover design by Steve Bassindale and Megan Trudell

The Socialist Workers Party is one of an international grouping of socialist organisations:
- **Australia:** International Socialists, PO Box A338 Sydney South
- **Belgium:** Socialisme International, Rue Lovinfosse 60, 4030 Grivengée, Belgium
- **Britain:** Socialist Workers Party, PO Box 82, London E3
- **Canada:** International Socialists, PO Box 339, Station E, Toronto, Ontario M6H 4E3
- **Cyprus:** Ergatiki Demokratia, PO Box 7280, Nicosia
- **Denmark:** Internationale Socialister, Postboks 642, 2200 København N, Denmark
- **France:** Socialisme International, BP 189, 75926 Paris Cedex 19
- **Greece:** Organosi Sosialisliki Epanastasi, c/o Workers Solidarity, PO Box 8161, Athens 100 10, Greece
- **Holland:** International Socialists, PO Box 9720, 3506 GR Utrecht
- **Ireland:** Socialist Workers Party, PO Box 1648, Dublin 8
- **New Zealand:** International Socialist Organization, PO Box 6157, Dunedin, New Zealand
- **Norway:** Internasjonale Socialisterr, Postboks 5370, Majorstua, 0304 Oslo 3
- **Poland:** Solidarność Socjalistyczna, PO Box 12, 01-900 Warszawa 118
- **South Africa:** Socialist Workers Organisation, PO Box 18530, Hillbrow 2038, Johannesberg
- **United States:** International Socialist Organisation, PO Box 16085, Chicago, Illinois 60616
- **Zimbabwe:** International Socialists, PO Box 6758, Harare

Contents

Lindsey German is a member of the Socialist Workers Party. She edits the monthly magazine, *Socialist Review.*

She has also written *Sex, Class and Socialism*, a widely read title now in its second edition

What is class?

Two children born on the same day can expect to live totally different lives depending on the class to which they belong. Their class background will have a much greater influence on their future development than any supposed intelligence, how hard they work at school, or any other subjective factor. A working class child will from birth experience worse and more cramped conditions, whether in hospital or at home. He or she will face, while an infant, a much greater prospect of death, of serious illness, or of suffering an accident in or around the home. Home itself will be much smaller, with the child sharing its bedroom with brothers or sisters. Play space will be a tiny garden or balcony or even the street. School will be overcrowded, housed in buildings which are in a poor state of repair.

For the children of the ruling class—and of a good section of the middle classes as well—the picture is very different. Their entry into life could not be more pampered. Born in private hospitals which are like hotels, brought up in houses which afford enough space for nannies and playrooms, which have substantial grounds, these children are given every advantage. Their health is on average much better than that of their working class counterparts, their chance of accident or disease much lower. Their schools are like palaces compared with the state schools most children have to attend. The ruling class child will attend a school with

7

acres of playing fields, swimming pools and tennis courts, well equipped libraries, language laboratories and facilities for music.

This childhood inequality is preparation—essential preparation—for an adulthood where most of one's life chances and choices are curtailed or at least severely constrained by the class from which an individual comes. Higher education qualifications, jobs and careers, income, where you live, where you shop, are in the vast majority of cases decided by class. Again, chances of accident or illness increase the further down the social scale you are. And although money can't buy health, it can make a difference. The poor—especially men—are likely to die younger than the rich.

That these differences exist is perfectly obvious to millions of people. Sayings such as, 'There's one law for the rich and one for the poor', sum up the feeling that some individuals get treated differently because they have more money, power and influence. That we 'live in a class society' is a common view. Most people also understand that they get treated very differently from their bosses. If they are manual workers they have to clock in, have regimented short breaks for meal times, often have to work overtime, and receive low wages and short holidays in return. White collar workers may sometimes have more flexibility, but they too will be increasingly supervised and forced to work harder for low pay.

Managers and bosses, on the other hand, are featherbedded: as a matter of course they gain company cars with free petrol, tax relief on private schools and other middle class perks, much longer holidays than workers and substantial pensions—usually amounting to much more than the average wage—when they retire. They claim that they deserve such cushioning because they work harder. But the majority work fewer hours than most manual workers, and included in their work time are such things as reading the newspapers on the way to work or going for three hour 'business lunches' paid for by expenses—both of which would be regarded as leisure pursuits by most workers.

The difference between classes in the world of work is perhaps the most noticeable aspect of people's lives, and certainly the one which determines so many of the factors—such as housing or health—which exist outside of paid work:

Those groups of men and women who experience the most adverse working conditions, the longest working hours, the most socially disruptive and personally wearing industrial routines, and who experience the lowest degree of job security and control—are characteristically less well paid than are other groups who produce less in easier and more certain conditions. Manual workers in particular work on average longer hours, do more shift work, have tighter controls on the content and timing of their work, and have a higher propensity to work in conditions that are noisier, subject to greater temperature extremes and supported by lower quality provision of canteens and lavatories, than do white collar and managerial staff.

At the same time they are more subject to industrial accidents, shorter holidays, smaller pensions, less secure earnings, greater unemployment and a quite different level and pattern of earnings during their working life—one that peaks early and declines into poverty in old age, unprotected by the increments and occupational pensions characteristic of middle management and state employed professionals.[1]

Housing is fairly rigidly segregated by class. Council estates, private estates of two or three bedroomed terraces or semi-detached houses, and rows of terraced houses are almost exclusively working class. The middle classes are much more likely to live in substantial houses with their own grounds. The rich live either in exclusive suburbs or the rich residential areas of London such as Knightsbridge, Mayfair or Belgravia. When mediated through class, home ownership is far less widespread than it might first appear, with only three quarters of even skilled workers having a mortgage, and that figure falling to well under 50 percent for the unskilled.

Whereas in 1992 a total of 87 percent of professionals and 90 percent of employers and managers either had a mortgage or owned a house outright, this fell to 75 percent for skilled manual workers, 73 percent for junior non-manual, 55 percent for semi-skilled manual workers and only 46 percent for unskilled manual workers.[2]

The story can be repeated in virtually every area of life. In general the poorer you are and the more routine your job is, the more likely you are to be sick, suffer from various diseases and die younger than your better off counterparts in professional or managerial jobs. This is most clearly true among manual workers but even among routine white collar workers evidence

9

suggests that class and work affect health. A study of stress levels among civil servants in London demonstrated that it was not high level executives who were most likely to suffer from ill health caused by pressure of work, but those who worked beneath them: 'The lowest grades—messengers and support staff—are three times more likely to die over a ten year period than senior administrators with high pressure jobs and they have six times more sick leave, although they are not poor or deprived by any absolute standard', according to the *Financial Times*.[3]

The possession of material goods differs widely between classes. While 52 percent of professionals and 41 percent of managers and employers possess home computers, only 33 percent of other non-manual workers do, and this falls to 27 percent of skilled and 21 percent of unskilled manual workers. A mere 4 percent of unskilled manual workers have a dishwasher, while 41 percent of professionals do. Professionals and managers are above the average in virtually every category of ownership of consumer durables.[4] Whereas 40 percent of those in classes D and E have no annual holiday, 80 percent of ABs have at least one holiday and around a fifth have three or more holidays a year.[5]

Quality of life is also determined by class. Professional and managerial groups are nearly twice as likely to go for a restaurant meal (excluding fast food) than semi-skilled or unskilled workers. While the average attendance at cinemas is 33 percent across the population, among the professional and managerial classes it is 46 percent. As the government publication *Social Trends* commented, 'People in social class AB participated more frequently in most of the [leisure] activities…than those in the other social classes.'[6]

Share ownership—supposedly the sign of a more egalitarian society as individuals have bought shares in their own companies or in the privatised businesses of the 1980s—also reflects class background. A survey carried out at the end of the 1980s revealed that 'those in the professional socio-economic group were seven times more likely to own shares than those from the unskilled manual group'.[7] Professionals are twice as likely as intermediate and junior non-manual grades to own shares.

Underpinning all these different forms of inequality is one simple fact: that the distribution of wealth is grossly unequal in capitalist society. The most wealthy 1 percent own 27 percent of the wealth, the most wealthy 5 percent own half of all wealth, the most wealthy quarter of the population own 80 percent of all wealth and the bottom 50 percent in society own only 7 percent of the wealth.[8] These figures are almost certainly an underestimate of the real wealth owned by the richest in society. Figures tend not to account for benefits in kind (for example from expense accounts), private health contributions from employers, untaxed property income and undistributed profits which will go to shareholders in the future.[9]

Inheritance plays a large part in determining who owns property, with women owning 40 percent of all private wealth even though their participation in business and the higher professions is at nowhere near that level.[10] What family and economic circumstances you are born into still plays the major part in determining where you end up. If everything else was equal and everyone was offered the same opportunities in life, then only 3 percent of sons from families in the top social groups would have found jobs within the same groups. One survey shows that, in reality, 40 percent did.[11] Another recent survey demonstrated that 'sons from managerial/professional families are getting on for three times as likely to end up in managerial/professional occupations themselves as are sons from semi-skilled and unskilled manual fathers. They are less than a third as likely to end up in this lowest group.'[12]

This inequality is reinforced by the way in which the upper classes and at least some of the middle classes use their wealth: they buy entry into schools which automatically give their children an even greater advantage than their superior wealth already gives them. The networks of family and friends work at this level to ensure that the children of the rich and powerful are helped into privileged jobs and have contacts to smooth their way throughout their careers. School, university and club are all part of the social structure which helps these people get on.

You would have to be wilfully blind or ignorant not to notice at least some of these inequalities. While open apologists for the system claim that the success of the rich is due to their own abilities—or, in the case of inherited wealth, is 'deserved' because of 'breeding'—the vast majority of people do recognise that there is something deeper and more structured which allows this inequality to continue.

Yet as we approach the end of the 20th century, there is a

11

growing consensus at the top of society that 'we are all middle class' and that notions of class divisions are outmoded. Even if class is no longer taken to have disappeared completely, it is certainly viewed by many people as a division which is on its way out. Definitions of the working class almost always exclude the bulk of white collar workers and therefore conclude that the working class is shrinking in size and influence. Explanations of inequality tend to focus on a prosperous mass above a deprived 'underclass' or to express social divisions in terms of a 'two thirds, one third' society—two thirds of whose members have some stake in prosperity, the other third being denied it.

The assumption is that there are extremes at both ends—the fat cats like Cedric Brown, former chief executive of British Gas, at the top of the scale and the dispossessed and unemployed of the 'underclass' at the bottom of the scale. There are periodically spates of articles in the press along the theme of 'we're all middle class now'. One recent example included within the middle class such unlikely figures as the Duchess of York and the multi-millionaire rock star Mick Jagger.[13] For a society where people talk about class and often feel themselves to be part of a particular class, definitions and understanding of what it is are remarkably blurred.

Perhaps this is because the popular view of class is that it is something to do with lifestyles, income or status. People define their class position by whether their parents were manual workers or what kind of accent they have. Class is seen through surface appearances, which depend very much on a view of lifestyles which seem to cut across class. Everyone seems to have a car, a mortgage, a personal pension plan, even though substantial minorities have access to none of these things. Nor are they just the 'underclass': for example, a full third of households in Britain have no access to a car and this rises to 40 percent in London.[14]

The mass production of culture and the development of an effective monopoly in certain areas mean that there is a constant attempt to portray certain habits as universal. So shopping at Sainsbury's, for example, is seen as something which involves all classes. Going to the cinema, or on a trip to a theme park, or playing computer games, seems to appeal across the class divide. Even Princess Diana takes her children to an amusement park and listens to music on a Walkman. Children from the most expensive public schools will occasionally eat at McDonald's, even if their usual food is somewhat more exclusive. All of this serves to hide or at least confuse class divisions. We are not told what sort of car people own, how many hours different people have to work to afford a trolley full of groceries at Sainsbury's, whether 'happy family' life is eased by being able to afford to employ a nanny. Historian Eric Hobsbawm's opinion that, 'the difference between the owner of a Volkswagen Beetle and the owner of a Mercedes was far less than that between the owner of any car and the owner of no car',[15] is a particularly crass example of this approach, at a time when the vast majority of working people not only cannot afford a Mercedes but in this country cannot afford a new car of any description.[16]

However, there is a particularly important political assumption here. The identification of lifestyles with class helps to strengthen the argument that the working class is disappearing. Today when sociologists or journalists refer to the 'old working class' they conjure up images of male manual workers in cloth caps and dungarees—as if this image ever represented all workers. Since the majority manifestly do not conform to this particular superficial image, we are told that therefore they are not working class or that the working class is declining. The same people do not, of course, conjure up similar images of men in waistcoats and bowler hats and conclude, since they no longer exist, that the middle class has disappeared.

But judging people by how they dress, where they shop or whether they have a sauce bottle on the kitchen table only focuses on surface appearances and can do nothing to explain the underlying social relations which exist inside capitalist society. This approach has become particularly common in recent years since the development of postmodern theory. The message is that everything is completely subjective, that you are what you wear or eat; politics equals identity—which means individual identity is defined through designer clothes or other consumer 'choices', rather than any form of collective identity. Identity politics are now held to be more important than class politics, with greater significance being given to whether one is female, black or gay and lesbian than to differences of class. Cultural preferences or consumerism are regarded as transcending class differences, being solely decided within the realm of the individual.

The same is true of definitions of class which focus on status—the idea that people's position in society is defined by a pecking

13

order into which everyone slots. This might tell you that everyone has a place, but it doesn't tell you why everyone has a place, and why some are higher up the hierarchy than others, or why some have power and others don't. Nor does it reveal where the interests of most people lie—do they lie in kicking those below them and ingratiating themselves with those above, or do they lie with those who may be slightly above or below in 'status' terms but who have overriding interests in common?

None of these subjective approaches really help in defining class, because they start with distribution and consumption, with the outcome of an unequal class society, rather than with what creates class society in the first place. Following in the tradition of the sociologist Max Weber they are derived from the way people behave.

If we want to understand how and why groups of people form classes at different points in history then we have to turn to the economic and social factors underpinning society. We have to see class as a relationship which is social, as opposed to individual. It does not depend in the first instance on how people feel about what class they are in, but on their objective relationship to what Karl Marx called the means of production (factories, machinery and so on). This analysis, developed by Marx and Frederick Engels in the 1840s, remains the only way of cutting a path through the vast number of subjective views of class and developing an understanding of why classes act as they do.

In present day society, Marx's approach that classes are defined by their relationship to the means of production means that the two major classes are defined by their position in the process of exploitation under capitalism, or by who is the exploiter and who is exploited. Marx and Engels' view was that historical development and change were the outcome of various struggles between different classes. It was absolutely central to them that 'the history of all hitherto existing society is the history of class struggles'.[17]

This meant that they were able to see social change not as a random series of unconnected events but as the product of a struggle between different classes for control of the wealth produced in that particular society. It did not matter that this struggle between the classes was 'now hidden, now open', that sometimes there didn't seem to be much struggle or, alternately, that what struggles were taking place didn't seem to have much to do with class.

14

As Marx and Engels wrote elsewhere, 'All struggles within the state, the struggle between democracy, aristocracy and monarchy, the struggle for the franchise etc, etc, are merely the illusory forms...in which the real struggles of the different classes are fought out among one another'.[18]

This class struggle resulted in two possible conclusions: 'either in a revolutionary reconstitution of society at large, or in the common ruin of the contending classes'.[19] Either the antagonisms resolved themselves by a new class breaking through and establishing its own rule—as happened for example in England with the civil war and revolution in the 17th century—or society went backwards with the collapse of both the old ruling class and its challenger—as happened with the fall of the Roman Empire.

The development of capitalism brought into being two major contending classes—the bourgeoisie and the proletariat. They were defined on the one hand by their ownership of the means of production, and on the other hand by their need to sell their labour power in order to survive. People who once earned their living in very different ways—peasants, small businessmen or craftsmen—found themselves more and more under pressure as the capitalist system developed. A tiny number became part of the bourgeoisie—the factory owners and capitalists—while the vast majority were pushed towards the working class, as this became the way that increasing numbers had to earn their livelihood.

Capitalism revolutionises all that has gone before. It creates big cities, centralises production, destroys all the old ways of working as its productive forces sweep everything before them. Societies which existed more or less unchanged for thousands of years have been rapidly destroyed once they have come into contact with the capitalist mode of production.

This is why Marx and Engels could write, 'Of all the classes that stand face to face with the bourgeoisie today, the proletariat alone is a really revolutionary class. The other classes decay and finally disappear in the face of modern industry, the proletariat is its special and essential product'.[20]

What is more, they continued, the proletariat is a revolutionary class which has to act collectively in order to change the world, because to make a workers' revolution it is necessary to overthrow not just a part of but the whole system of exploitation.

Marx and Engels are making two points here: that the working class is a potentially revolutionary class, and that the

15

only way a revolution can take place is through the working class acting together to seize control of the means of production and establish a society based not on private property but on socialised production for the benefit of the whole of society.

The Marxist historian G E M de Ste Croix, in his book about class struggle in the ancient world, has defined class in the following way:

> Class (essentially a relationship) is the collective social expression of the fact of exploitation, the way in which exploitation is embodied in a social structure. By *exploitation* I mean the appropriation of part of the product of the labour of others: in a commodity-producing society this is the appropriation of what Marx called 'surplus value'.
>
> A class (a particular class) is a group of persons in a community identified by their position in the whole system of social production, defined above all according to their relationship (primarily in terms of the degree of ownership or control) to the conditions of production (that is to say, the means and labour of production) and to other classes.[21]

It is important to understand that this is an *objective* relationship; the actual class position of individuals depends not on what they feel about which class they are in, but whether they are forced to sell their labour power in order to survive. Class position is not therefore the same as class consciousness; workers are still workers even if they vote Tory, buy their council houses or own a few shares. This basic point is often lost on those many commentators who confuse the interests of the working class with its actual consciousness. They often claim that since Marx said the working class is a revolutionary class, and since for most of the time most workers hold ideas which are very far from revolutionary, then Marx must have been wrong on this point.

But there is clearly a difference between the interests of working class people and the ideas that they might hold at a particular time. Marx makes this point time and again. His view of the working class is not that it is all revolutionary all the time but that its condition of exploitation—its relationship to the means of production, to use the term which defines class—will lead it towards a certain form of class struggle and creates a tendency for it to act in a certain way. In *The Holy Family*, one of the earliest collaborations between Marx and Engels, they write:

> It is not a question of what this or that proletarian, or even the whole proletariat, at the moment *regards* as its aim. It is a question of *what the proletariat is*, and what, in accordance with this *being*, it will historically be compelled to do.[22]

Starting from this approach allows Marx to make the distinction between the working class as it is—warts and all—and what it is capable of becoming.

This is important because it allows us to understand two things. The first is that, however unrevolutionary or passive working class people might be at a particular time, the basic contradiction inside capitalist society is the fact of their exploitation by a minority class and that this itself will tend to lead to conflict at certain times. Historically the main conflict has been over how great a share of the surplus produced will go to the people who produce it, and how much to those who own the means of production. At times there may be little overt conflict over such questions; at other times such conflicts will flare up into big struggles. Class is a dynamic relationship where workers are created by the process of exploitation, which draws in more and more of the population to the production of profits for the capitalists. In turn, the situation they find themselves in leads over a period of time to them seeing themselves as workers and developing a certain set of ideas and attitudes in common with other workers.

The second important point to be drawn from this understanding of class is that it allows for the intervention of socialists and militants—the subjective role of individuals—in developing class struggle and fostering class consciousness. If the working class is potentially a class which is led to fight against the system then the role of revolutionaries is to help bring out that potential.

Many even on the left take a different attitude to class, stressing class as an unchanging sociological fact and class consciousness as something fixed and determined. So only those people who think of themselves as workers and act in certain ways in which workers are 'supposed' to act are working class. It is a view which cannot assimilate changes inside the working class and has been one of the major underpinnings of theories which have bid 'farewell to the working class' with such regularity. For example, women bank workers are about as far from the stereotypical image of the male manual worker as possible—so it is assumed that they cannot be working class. Some women bank workers may see themselves as middle class—so they cannot be workers either. This approach can only lead to utterly pointless speculation about whether such and such an individual can be considered a worker. This in its turn helps to confuse any serious analysis of class. The real point is that even if a worker cuts across class stereotypes by, for example, listening to opera, there is something more fundamental which defines him or her than one particular leisure pursuit: whether or not he or she is forced to sell his or her labour power in order to live.

If the view of the working class outlined above is essentially one which sees the working class as a backward and unchanging mass out of which a handful of gifted individuals are able to emerge, there is another view which seems to mirror it. This second view differentiates among workers, locating workers who are in unions, for example, as more advanced than those who are not. However, the idea of fixing on a particular 'vanguard'—in whichever way it is defined—leads to defining workers not by what they are, or what their life situation leads them to be, but rather by what they think. Class therefore becomes something which is not primarily defined by the relationship of a group of people to the means of production, but by how they subjectively see themselves. As the historian E P Thompson puts it in the introduction to his book *The Making of the English Working Class*:

> Class happens when some men, as a result of common experiences (inherited or shared), feel and articulate the identity of their interests as between themselves, and as against other men whose interests are different from (and usually opposed to) theirs.[23]

The problem with this formulation and ones like it is that they accept half the analysis of class—that in the process of becoming and acting like a class, members of that class develop a consciousness, a set of ideas, because they are members of a particular class. But it is also true that workers can act as workers against the bosses without being properly conscious of themselves as workers. This is why Marx made a distinction between the working class 'in itself' and the working class 'for itself'—between a class which exists objectively and one which comes to consciousness as a class.[24]

To avoid a static view of class—and indeed of workers'

consciousness as part of a class—it is necessary to have a sense of dynamism and change within the class struggle. Otherwise it is all too easy to accept that a set of rigid views will be held by most 'backward' workers, and an equally rigid set of views—if more progressive—will be held by 'vanguard' workers. It is only a short step from this to deciding that if the 'vanguard'—print or engineering workers for example—is in decline, then the working class itself is in decline also. [25]

There is another problem we face when dealing with class today. The structure of capitalist society is clearly more complicated than simply being divided into two diametrically opposed classes. Firstly, there is a substantial 'middle class'—often put at 15 to 20 percent of the population; secondly, the working class itself seems so divided on grounds of gender, nation or race that it cannot be talked about as one cohesive class.

Capitalism destroyed a whole number of the old classes as it developed, partly through machinery making their skills and knowledge obsolete, partly through competition from big capital driving them out of business. This pushed more and more people towards the working class, and therefore towards one of the major contending classes. However this did not mean the total disappearance of those layers between the two big classes. Marx understood this when he wrote the piece on 'Classes' which makes up the final unfinished chapter of *Capital* volume III, and when he talked about the complexity of the picture of classes in England, by far the most developed capitalist country at the time which had therefore seen the decline or disappearance of a number of old classes to a greater degree than elsewhere:

> Even [in England] the stratification of classes does not appear in its pure form. Middle and intermediate strata even here obliterate lines of demarcation everywhere. However, this is immaterial for our analysis. We have seen that the continual tendency and law of development of the capitalist mode of production is more and more to divorce the means of production from labour, and more and more to concentrate the scattered means of production into large groups, thereby transforming labour into wage labour and the means of production into capital.[26]

Capitalism acted to make the two major classes more universal and to wipe out other classes. This did not mean extinction for the petty bourgeoisie or the professionals such as lawyers and doctors. Today the development of giant corporations, the spread of education, the need for a skilled, literate and numerate workforce means a big 'middle class' salariat.

However, if we accept the view of class as spelt out by Marx as meaning there are two major contending classes whose position and interests are defined by their relationship to the means of production, then that only takes us so far in our analysis of capitalist society today. Just as we have to look below the surface reality to understand the real relations of production, so we also have to try to understand the complexity of class society today. There may be obvious groups of people who fit into the categories of 'capitalist' or 'worker'. But there are also sizeable numbers who seem to fit neither definition. What is their role?

The aim of the following chapters is to try to provide some answers about the state of the working class—in what respect has it changed, where do the other classes fit in and does the working class have power in the modern world?

'The most revolutionary class'

'I f people still admit to being working class—and surveys suggest they frequently do—it is seldom the heroic working class of Marx that they have in mind. Increasingly, the working class is something that people come from. It is what most people's parents were. The working class is a starting point, from which we can measure the immensity of the distance we have travelled. The working class has been, as it were, evicted from history.'[1]

The sense that the working class belongs to the past is so pervasive that it is accepted almost without question. The declining, disappearing or dying working class has formed the basis of so many books, newspaper articles and university studies that it has become a cliché. The politics underpinning the policies of the two major parties rest on this assumption. The Tories with their talk about the 'classless society' and Thatcher's famous statement that 'there is no such thing as society' try to appeal to workers as individuals who are all supposedly desperate to enter the 'middle classes'. Labour accepts the argument that the old communities of the working class which created such strong electoral support for Labour are now gone and that most workers—apart from the unfortunate 'underclass'—can share in the prosperity of capitalist society.

These conclusions are drawn from two main sources. The first is the decline, in all the major capitalist countries, of manufacturing industry as a proportion of all industry, and the growth of services. Manufacturing output has in fact grown substantially even over the past 20 years—and even in Britain has stagnated rather than fallen. But because this growth has been accompanied by even bigger increases in productivity it has been possible to run down the manufacturing workforce and to increase service employment. One of the effects of this is to reduce the share of manufacturing as a proportion of overall wealth produced.[2] Alongside this has been a reduction in the number of blue collar manual workers and a massive growth in white collar work. Both have in fact been features of the second half of the 20th century (and there are many indications that this trend has been at work throughout the whole of the century). This alteration in the structure of the working class and the sort of work that people do has led to the conclusion that the working class as traditionally composed is shrinking and therefore cannot have the same social importance as it had previously.

This view is reinforced by the idea that some of these white collar workers or service workers may indeed be part of the working class but they no longer think like workers. They tend not to join unions, they almost never go on strike, and they define themselves by the world of consumption and leisure, not the world of production and work.

In addition, the alleged process of de-industrialisation in the advanced capitalist countries and the decline of certain industries further strengthens the nostalgic view that real jobs like mining and steelworking no longer exist, that nothing is any longer manufactured in countries like Britain and the jobs available to young people today are virtually worthless. 'Generation X' is never going to experience real work but is consigned to a future of 'McJobs' which are always going to be low status and badly organised. As one former miner said recently:

This country's going to be one massive theme park. You can

either be hot dog sellers or taxi drivers... What's happened in this country is that you've lost your industrial baselands. You've lost your steelworks, your dock labour schemes—you've even lost your docks and your shipbuilding. You've come away from industrial workers to white collar workers. Now that's not saying that white collar workers are less militant or less unionised, but inevitably, they don't live in communities.[3]

This picture of strong groups of male manual workers in 'Fordist' production line industries which dominated whole communities or even cities and regions remains embedded in working class memory. In the South Wales valleys up to 50 years ago virtually every male would end up working at the pit or the steelworks. The same was true in other regions of heavy industry— the north east, the central Scottish industrial belt, Yorkshire. Even the areas of the 'new' industries of the 1920s and 1930s which boomed throughout most of the inter-war depression years have now become victims of industrial destruction. West London's listed Hoover factory, for example, is now 'preserved' as a Tesco superstore.

So the memory is one of booming industry and goods being produced, of workers feeling a sense of collective purpose, which has now been lost to be replaced by '[an entire country] identified with an earlier phase of industry, such as Great Britain, [which has been] largely de-industrialised, turning into living or dying museums of a vanished past, which entrepreneurs exploited, with some success, as tourist attractions.'[4]

But it is a memory which is at best partial. For the industries and jobs which we remember as traditional or typical are themselves relatively recent arrivals on the scene. Capitalism is characterised by the constant revolutionising of the means of production. This means that from its earliest inception one of its key features has been restructuring: once dynamic industries go into decline while new ones spring up. Alongside these have gone newly developed towns and regions, new habits of work, further ancillary industries which serve the new industries and—most importantly—a new working class. This process is as old as capitalism itself. The basis of much of the Industrial Revolution— which began in the 18th century and ushered in the era of industrial capitalism—was the textile industry. The Lancashire cotton towns, with Manchester at their centre, grew at fantastic speed as labour was sucked in from the surrounding countryside, from agricultural and mining workers as far away as Cornwall and from the impoverished Irish peasantry.

A new working class was created, often composed of women prepared to work for relatively low wages. Every working class account of the development of that industry contains heartfelt reminiscences of the previous age—an age where weavers were men, where manufacturing work took place within the home, not within the satanic mills of the cotton towns, and where people were not driven to live in city slums. Yet resistance to industrialisation and to the conditions of work and living—which partly motivated the mass working class Chartist movement of the 1830s and 1840s—did not prevent the spread of the textile industry or of the big cities. Instead by the middle of the 19th century, following the misery of the 1840s and the defeat of Chartism, came the acceptance and consolidation of certain living patterns. At this time too came the move away from the predominance of textiles towards forms of heavy industry which still characterise many people's view of British industry.

The development of this new production was based on exports to other parts of the world. So the share of exports of cotton yarn and goods fell from 50.8 percent of the economy in 1830 to 35.8 percent in 1870.[5] The expansion of heavy industrial exports went in the opposite direction: 'In 1840-2 [the new capital goods] formed about 11 percent of the value of our exports of manufactures, by 1857-9 22 percent, by 1882-4 27 percent. Between 1840-2 and 1857-9 coal exports rose from less than three quarters of a million pounds to over three million, iron and steel exports from about three million to well over thirteen million.'[6]

Production of iron, steel and coal rose dramatically in this period of industrial expansion, with iron and coal production trebling between 1850 and 1870, and steel increasing from 49,000 tons to 147,000 tons over the same period. Already by 1880 the number of coal miners in Britain stood at half a million and by the outbreak of the First World War in 1914 it had reached 1.2 million.[7]

This change in the structure of British capitalism created the 'classic' view of the working class—almost exclusively male, working in heavy industry, part of a community in pit villages or steel towns or even in the big railway towns such as Crewe, Swindon or Derby. It was not, of course, the picture for even a majority of workers. It would seem that:

> While Britain was proverbially known as the 'workshop of the world', it was—rather surprisingly—never the case that the majority of its workforce was employed in manufacturing and related industries, so far as the existing statistics—which are, admittedly, fairly patchy prior to the mid-19th century—are able to show...total employment in manufacturing industry never, at any time, amounted to one half of the employed population, although it was, until recently, the largest single sector.[8]

While most of the workforce was classified as manual labour in the second half of the 19th century,[9] it would be wrong to equate these workers with manufacturing industry.

They covered the whole range of sectors from manufacturing to agriculture. So the two largest employers of female labour were textiles—usually relatively well paid and well organised—and domestic service, which was classified as semi-skilled but was often drudgery of the worst sort. Domestic workers were virtually unorganisable, subject to terrible conditions and poor wages.

Agricultural workers also made up a large proportion of the workforce. Three times as many people worked in agriculture than in textiles in 1851 and by the end of the century in 1891 it still employed more than any other single industrial group.[10] And industrialisation was heavily concentrated. Workers in London were often service workers and there was a strong bias towards casualisation. The London dockers were casual workers, and there was a whole range of occupations—often involving women workers—which operated on this basis, including sellers of various street goods, seamstresses, hatters and glovemakers.[11]

The working class was not at all homogeneous—its attitudes, ideas and behaviour varied according to particular workers' recent history, the size of their workplaces and the way they worked. For the most part, none of these groups of workers developed especial militancy until the late 1880s and again in the period of the Great Unrest from 1910 to 1914. And when the strikes broke out in the 1880s which led to the formation of the new—general as opposed to skilled—unions, their very character demonstrated that they were revolts by those regarded as the least advanced among the working class. The strikes of match girls, dockers, gas workers, pickle, jam and sweet factory workers were all organised and led by women, Irish immigrants and the unskilled. These were the supposedly unorganisable.

The groups considered well organised today such as shipyard workers or engineers were noted for, at best, very narrow and craftist sectional strikes.

The development of heavy industry marked the heyday of British capitalism and the vast export markets showed the extent of the British Empire and its influence throughout the world. However, in the last decades of the 19th century, Britain faced increasing competition on the world market, especially from the US and Germany, in areas such as steel and manufactured goods. The core British industries—textiles, steel, shipbuilding, railways—began their slow relative decline. Alongside this came a further restructuring of the working class.

While these industries retained a massive importance at least up to the First World War, they were joined by a whole number of others which not only produced new goods but tended to do so in a different way. For the first time, and following from industrial development in the United States, came mass production industries often geared to domestic consumer markets. These included goods such as typewriters and sewing machines. As the 20th century began, there were industries devoted to the production of cars and bicycles, or consumer goods for the home. These industries tended to be organised on production line techniques, which created a division of labour within the manufacture of, say, a motor car which was designed to get the maximum productivity from workers by forcing them to repeat identical tasks. The time it took to perform each task was measured, and speed-up became a constant pressure in such jobs. The terms 'Fordism' (after the car manufacturer Henry Ford who opened up the first mass market in cars in the US) and 'Taylorism' (after the founder of 'scientific management', F W Taylor) both entered the language to describe a new form of organising industry which was to have a profound impact on the working class in the 20th century.

The change in British industry became most apparent in the inter-war years, as did the change in the working class. Miners in particular still played a very important role in the composition of the working class—still over 1 million at the time of the General Strike in 1926—but traditional British heavy industry had come out of the war severely weakened and was never really to recover. As the workforce grew overall, the relative weight of workers in these industries declined as a proportion of the whole.

What sort of jobs and what sort of workers replaced them? Firstly there were the 'new industries'—aircraft, cars, electrical goods. These could not have been in greater contrast to the old declining industries. The factories tended to be lighter and more modern. Work was usually organised on production line techniques. These new industries sprang up in different parts of the country from the old coal and steel and related industries. Oxford, the West Midlands, especially Coventry, and parts of London became boom areas even during most of the 1930s Depression. The workers in the factories were 'new' workers: young people from rural areas who had few prospects on the land or in local industries. Many women who were not prepared to go into domestic service as their mothers or grandmothers had done were attracted by the relatively 'clean' conditions of the new factories, as well as their amenities such as social clubs. In addition, there were masses of ex-miners, especially from South Wales after the pits there closed. They often walked to Slough or the west London suburbs to find work. Similarly in Coventry and Oxford there were workers from Scotland, the north east and other depressed areas who had to travel to find work. It was these workers—rather than the new 'green' workers as one Communist organiser described them in the 1930s—who tended to be central to trying to build union organisation, such as it was in those Depression years.[12]

In addition to new manufacturing there was also the increase in shop work in the inter-war years, responding to a huge expansion of retail outlets, with a growth by two thirds of tobacconists shops, of two and a half times in the number of confectionery shops and a trebling in the number of shops selling medical preparations.[13]

The other area of industry which began to make an impact on the structure of the working class was the growth of clerical work. It is remarkable how the job went from being a respectable, almost exclusively male and very elitist occupation to being the favoured job of young working class women who were able to gain any qualifications. It is also remarkable how quickly it became subject to the same sorts of pressure and even conditions of work as many non-clerical jobs. The typing pool, the telephone exchange with dozens of operators, the need for a whole section of workers called 'filing clerk', testified to the way that 'Taylorist' methods were encroaching on a section of workers once regarded as privileged and outside the working class.

27

The expansion of clerical work before the Second World War was as nothing compared with its growth afterwards, which continues today. However, it—like its counterpart in manufacturing—is constantly being restructured. Whole areas such as comptometer operating or shorthand typing no longer exist as they did 50 years ago. They have been replaced by jobs such as word processor operators or colour photocopier operators which have revolutionised occupations like banking. Alongside this goes a constant process of training, retraining, and a replenishing of older workers with newer, fresher and (in the eyes of the capitalists) more adaptable ones. This change in clerical work has been matched by innovation in shop work, factory production and every other area of working life comparable to the sorts of changes in the work process, and therefore in the working class, which have occurred since capitalism began.

In the second half of the 20th century there have been still further changes, with a more dramatic move away from manufacturing to services, as manufacturing industry has become more and more productive and so shed more and more jobs, while many services have remained much more labour intensive. At the same time a whole 'shadow system of production' has grown with paperwork existing alongside the actual production process—bringing with it a whole new workforce.[14] Areas such as finance or sales which play a large part in the distribution of manufactured goods are examples of this tendency.

Each of these broad trends needs to be looked at in turn if we are to understand what is happening to work and workers today.

The manufacturing/services divide

Movement throughout the 20th century has been away from the manufacturing section of industry and towards services. The growth of service industry shows no sign of being reversed in Britain. Employment in industry and manufacturing (including areas such as extraction of raw materials) stood at 43.9 percent of the workforce in 1901, 47.8 percent in 1961 and 30.6 percent in 1987. Services, on the other hand, went from 30.2 percent in 1901 to 41.2 percent in 1961 to 68 percent (35.5 percent in commerce and 32.5 percent in public and other services) by 1987.[15] The pace of decline of manufacturing in Britain has intensified even more in recent years. Now the manufacturing sector accounts for only about a fifth of industry.[16]

Eric Hobsbawm has described the loss of manufacturing industry in Britain in the early 1980s, when a quarter of manufacturing was lost, as a 'veritable industrial holocaust'.[17] The closure of nearly all the coal mines in Britain can be seen in the same way. But while the general picture seems to be of the loss of 'real' jobs to be replaced by 'heritage theme park' jobs, the nature of the service industries and the sorts of jobs which have been created is rather different.

Service jobs are not just waitressing, hairdressing or working in McDonald's. Many service jobs would be considered 'old' working class jobs. Transport workers, postal workers, dockers and telecom engineers all fall into the services category. They have always made up a substantial proportion of the workforce even in the heyday of manufacturing—as we see above from the nearly one third engaged in service industry at the turn of the present century. A sizeable number of such jobs are white collar and some of them are reasonably skilled—like bank workers—but there are many service jobs which are not in this category. If one of the sociological criteria of the working class is of a group of people who get their hands dirty, then many service workers fit this description. Kwikfit workers who fit new car exhausts or drivers and warehouse workers who load machinery onto lorries are as likely to fit the traditional pattern of a 'worker' as someone who works on the assembly line at Ford, yet they are included in the figures for service sector workers. Service jobs in some areas are also subject to automation, for example in modern supermarkets.

It is hard to see any fundamental or useful distinction between a whole number of service jobs and those in manufacturing.

> Restaurant labour, which cooks, prepares, assembles, serves, cleans dishes and utensils, etc, carries on tangible production just as much as labour employed in many another manufacturing process; the fact that the consumer is sitting nearby at a counter or table is the chief distinction, in principle, between this industry and those food processing industries which are classified under 'manufacturing'. Laundry workers, workers in cleaning and pressing establishments, workers in automobile repair shops and in machine servicing or repair work of other sorts perform the same sort of work as many workers in manufacturing industries.[18]

29

Services have grown as capitalism itself has grown. The encroachment of the market into more and more areas of life means that services which were once performed outside the area of wage labour are now transformed into jobs in service industries. Cooking, cleaning and personal grooming, plus childcare, were all jobs which at one time would have been performed in and around the home as part of the general running of the home and certainly would not have commanded a wage. Transformed into commodities, these tasks are now performed outside the home as wage labour.

In addition, as industrial production develops so does the need for more service industries which sustain it. For every job manufacturing cars on a production line at Ford, there will be jobs matching it in services. Components such as gearboxes have to be transported to the factory. The finished cars themselves have to be transported to showrooms or to ports. Without this transport the commodity produced is of little use. Indeed there is an argument that such jobs form a part of manufacturing industry, since without them the production of the commodity in question is not complete.

A whole number of other jobs help to maintain manufacturing production—the transport of workers to and from work, feeding them in canteens, doing the paperwork related to sales or finance which is so central to the marketing of commodities today. In an advanced capitalist society even jobs which have a much more distant relationship to manufacturing industry—for example in education or healthcare—are arguably essential to the production process. This is certainly true in that capitalism needs a literate, educated, healthy and relatively long lived workforce in order to develop the productivity of labour and squeeze the maximum amount of surplus value from its workers.

Even the notorious McDonald's jobs or stacking shelves in massive supermarkets should be seen in the context of the production process. Shift working, 'flexibility', women going out to work in massive numbers, have all helped to create a 'services infrastructure' of drive-in restaurants and shops, open seven days a week, where long hours once spent in the kitchen by housewives are replaced by cheap takeaway meals or microwave 'ready meals' which can be prepared in minutes by women who have to work outside the home as well as care for children.

The reality of women working outside the home is, of course, not new. In the Lancashire cotton districts in the 19th century women went to work, and they found that here too a network of childminders, pudding shops and the like sprang up to serve these women and their families.[19] A report from the 1860s noted that 'a very large class of women derive their maintenance entirely by providing for the wants of the mill hands'.[20] The difference today is that these jobs, then often arranged through friends or neighbours on an informal basis and for a small cash payment, are now organised as part of the production process. In general this makes the workers in them much easier to organise, more likely to think of themselves as workers and more likely to find themselves in an antagonistic relationship with their bosses than their counterparts in the last century.

Yet many people persist in the view that service jobs are somehow 'worth' less than their manufacturing counterparts. This view cannot really be sustained. There are service jobs which are useful to society as a whole (childcare for example), those which are useful to capital (including its whole distribution network of warehouses and supermarkets, without which no commodities could be sold) and many which are extremely profitable for the capitalists (McDonald's is one of the world's top companies). In what sense can these be seen as less 'useful' or less 'real' jobs than making a nuclear submarine or a Barbie doll?

It is worth remembering that there are still nearly 5 million manufacturing jobs, alongside 1.7 million in construction and 325,000 in energy and water supply.[21] By any standards this is still a substantial group of the 'old working class'. Indeed a quarter of all male workers are employed in manufacturing industry. These are very often concentrated in large workplaces where organisation is strong.

> In 1993, there were still over 1,000 manufacturing sites with more than 500 employees...notwithstanding the decline of manufacturing employment relative to the rest of the British workforce, its social weight still outweighs its numerical size (both in terms of its importance to the state of the economy as a whole and in overall levels of industrial action) and its workers still wield enormous potential muscle due to their strategic position at the point of production.[22]

Many service workers are traditionally organised 'old working class'—for example transport workers. If we add these to the growing numbers of the 'new working class' then we are talking of a bigger and more powerful working class than ever before.

What sort of jobs do we get today?

The most common response to the changes in work patterns in recent years is to claim that jobs as we know them are rapidly disappearing. According to this view the old male full time worker is being replaced by the new flexible, often female, worker. People now tend to work on fixed term contracts, in temporary jobs, and often on a part time basis. We are presented with an image of a workforce which—if permanently employed—is on annualised hours, totally dependent on the whim of their boss for whether they work or not, and which hours they are forced to work. For increasing numbers there seems to be a return to casualisation, to working if and when you can, as well as to homeworking as a means of making a living.

Perhaps because the picture is so often painted by journalists or academics—who themselves are some of the workers most likely to work from home, get involved in fixed term contracts or engage in job sharing—these jobs are shown as the work of the future. But in reality there has been a remarkably small shift in the patterns of work despite the decline of full time permanent jobs in certain parts of industry such as coal mining. Nor is there much evidence of a growing polarisation between a 'core' of well paid and secure workers and a 'periphery' of low skilled casualised and poorly paid workers who service the inner core.

The vast majority of workers are full time and permanent. Of a total of 21.9 million employees in September 1995 around 15.7 million were full time.[23] At around the same time there were about 1.5 million temporary workers—an increase of about 10 percent on a year earlier but still a small proportion of the whole.[24]

Flexibility is also greatly overestimated. In 1995 a total of 11.3 percent of full time workers and 8.5 percent of part time workers had flexible working hours. Since the vast majority of these worked what is known as 'flexitime'—a certain number of hours worked between say 8am and 7pm in a working day—this hardly amounts to the sort of 'flexible' working that we might expect from the term. It is flexible in the sense that people can come into or leave work relatively earlier or later and that they can miss their lunch break to 'gain' an hour. But the concept revolves around a core 9 to 5 working day. The majority of flexible workers are full time—again contrary to the popular picture—and flexible working is most common in areas where full time workers make up a big proportion of the workforce. So 'in banking, financial and business services around 18 percent of employees worked flexitime compared with 6 percent in the distribution, hotels and catering and repairs industries in spring 1994.'[25]

These are workers who prefer flexible work in order to miss the rush hour, or to get home when their children get home from school—they are not people whose work pattern is different in any essential from office workers not on flexitime. The same is true of many other 'flexible' workers. Included in this category, for example, are workers on a four and a half day week, those on a nine day fortnight and those with annualised working hours. The majority in all these categories are full time workers who again work a 'traditional' working week but who have gained half a day off on Friday (a common pattern in many engineering factories, for instance, especially since the engineering union's campaign for a 37 hour week in the late 1980s).

Only 0.1 percent of full time workers and 2.3 percent of part timers were involved in job sharing in the spring of 1995. Despite predictions that this could mark an important work pattern of the future, it seems to be of only very minority appeal. One probable reason why so few full time women workers job share is that it is only worth doing if the job is sufficiently well paid in the first place—and it therefore tends to be restricted to more professional jobs such as journalism or lecturing.

Homeworking too is less prevalent than is sometimes thought. A total of 0.7 million workers work from home, although this figure covers groups as diverse as farmers and piece workers. Around 4 in 10 are manual workers and one in six are employers or managers. A full three quarters of homeworkers either own their own business or work on their own account (as freelances, for example).[26] So the belief that computer technology will allow millions of workers to sit at a terminal and work from home does not seem to be borne out.

Although projections of future trends are not necessarily accurate, they certainly do not point to a major expansion of homeworking over the near future. A study of labour market flexibility which is based on the government's Labour Force Survey has concluded that 'the vast majority of British workers will still be in permanent full time jobs 10 years from now, with 6 percent employed on temporary contracts'.[27] It predicts that the number of temporary workers will grow by a million in the next ten years but that this will not represent a dramatic rise in the proportion of temporary workers in the workforce. So full time permanent workers will still compose 79.2 percent of all employees in 2005 compared with 82.1 percent today and 83.9 percent ten years ago.[28] The number of self employed is unlikely to change much, going from 3.3 million today to 3.6 million in 2005. The proportion of part time workers will increase by only 1 percent and will rise from 6 million to 6.7 million.[29]

All this points to a workforce and a working class which has lost none of its essential characteristics and which is still very far from being the sort of flexible workforce predicted.

Women workers

The most obvious single change in the working class during the 20th century has been the rise of the woman worker. Under represented in many of the 'old' industries, they are the majority in a whole number of areas today, many of which are in the expanding section of the workforce. This explains in part the unemployment rate among women being much lower than among men—7.2 percent in 1994 for women compared with 11.4 percent for men.[30] The jobs being created in most areas are more likely to be 'women's jobs'. Women accounted for not much less than 50 percent of employees in Britain in 1994, compared with 38 percent in 1971.[31] Although this represents a real step forward in terms of women's involvement in the workforce it is seen by many commentators on the structure of the working class as a step backwards. The reasons for these attitudes range from barely concealed male chauvinism—that women can simply never become organised in a way that male workers have traditionally been—to the familiar idea that their jobs cannot be 'real' jobs. They are, after all, white collar, service jobs and a high proportion of women workers are part time. These factors all make it impossible to equate women workers with their male counterparts—or so the myth goes. Let us look at the arguments in turn.

Part time workers

We cannot talk about the growth of part time work without talking about women. Women make up the bulk of part time workers—and the vast majority of part time women workers are also mothers or wives. Their jobs fit in around their family lives and very often around the demands of childcare. Today part time employment accounts for around a quarter of all jobs in Britain, with women taking up about 85 percent of them.[32]

Part time work has always been done by women because of their childcare responsibilities, but it really took off in Britain during the 1950s and 1960s, as a result of the economic expansion during the postwar boom. Women, as well as large numbers of immigrant workers, were pulled into paid work, even though they were married and had children. But because the state did not want to shoulder the burden of childcare the part time arrangement was one which suited, since mothers could fill their basic responsibilities for children at little cost to the state. It also suited many workers, since there was full employment in stable occupations, wages and living standards were rising steadily. The part time wage was often seen as an adjunct to the family income, rather than central to that income in its own right. Already by 1951 around 20 percent of married women were working, by the 1980s this figure stood at over 50 percent.[33]

The number of part time workers in the economy remains high. But the *growth* of part time work in the past decade has been much higher among men—from just over half a million in 1984 to just under a million now.[34] Women's part time employment in the same period went up from 5.4 million to 6.1 million, a much smaller proportional increase. Between 1984 and 1994 the number of male full time jobs actually fell, while the number of women working full time actually went up by 13 percent.[35] A substantial number of the full time jobs are now occupied by women with children. Until the 1980s, nearly all women who had any choice in the matter tended to return to work part time after having children, even if they had worked full time before. Now they are much more likely to go back into full time work after a relatively short period of maternity leave.

Amongst women whose first child was born in the late 1940s, only 5 percent returned to work *full time* within six months of the birth, a proportion which was little higher in the late 1970s… By the late 1980s, however, a woman who had been working full time when she became pregnant was just as likely to return to full time as to part time work. Since 1979…the proportion of women returning to work within nine months of the child's birth had increased from 25 percent to 45 percent. But even more strikingly, the proportion of mothers working *full time* within that period had increased much faster than the proportion working part time.[36]

These trends suggest a move by large numbers of women towards permanent full time employment regardless of whether they have children. There are other pointers to such a development—for example the increase in women going into higher education, gaining professional qualifications and the like. The image of women workers in marginal part time jobs to which they have no great commitment is less and less an accurate reflection of reality. This is even true of many part time women workers themselves.

The majority of women who work now work full time. Around 58 percent are on 30 hours or more a week. But even those who qualify as part timers vary greatly in terms of hours worked, commitment to the job, integration into the job and so on. For example, of the 1.7 million women working in clerical occupations, around half a million are part time.[37] But these workers are just as likely to be permanent and to see themselves as identical to full timers except for the amount of hours that they do. In the personal service industries or in shop work there is likely to be less identification with the job—and these are areas where the majority of women workers are part timers and there is a much greater tendency towards low skill and low wage work. Even here, however, there is pressure for workers to develop identification with the firm.

A study of workers at two branches of Maguires food stores in Swindon showed that employers have an assumption that 'labour supply is dependable. All members of staff had contracts. Even school students pushing trolleys around the car park on a Saturday afternoon were expected to sign a contract with the company… The ability to bring labour "on stream" to meet changes in customer demand presupposed a high degree of dependability and low absenteeism and good time keeping.'[38] This reinforces another basic fact about part time work: that if it is undertaken with full time workers, if there is some training and permanence in the job, then part time workers—although in general worse organised and lower paid than full timers—will tend to respond in the same way as their full time counterparts. This is even true when it comes to joining unions. The reverse is clearly true in small non-union workplaces or where workers see themselves in stop gap jobs.[39]

White collar workers

A quarter of all women work in clerical and secretarial work. The increase in white collar jobs has gone alongside the rise in service occupations, although there are many service jobs which are manual. There are also a substantial number of white collar jobs in manufacturing industry. However, if we add the quarter of all women in clerical and related jobs to women in other white collar jobs—in areas like health, education or welfare work, plus at least some sales work—then we are considering millions of white collar jobs.

The growth of white collar jobs throughout this century has been accompanied by two developments: the growing proportion of women in the workforce—which has tended to lead to these jobs being less valued and relatively low paid—and the decline in status of white collar work itself. Work which was once done by lower middle class males in Victorian times is now typically done by working class females. Clerical posts in the 19th century were in many ways more akin to managerial work today. The Arkwright family—the mill owners—'in 1801-4, employed only three clerks to look after 1,063 workers'.[40] The popular fictional clerks in the City of London—Bob Cratchit in Dickens's *Christmas Carol* or Charles Pooter in *The Diary of a Nobody* did not lead particularly comfortable lives but were still considered sufficiently removed from their manual working class counterparts to feel some sense of detachment. Clerical workers as male heads of the family could earn enough to perhaps live in a respectable suburb, to mix with other clerks and to see their job as having prospects and status. Harry Braverman argues that in the 19th century, 'in terms of function, authority, pay, tenure of employment (a clerical position was usually a lifetime post), prospects, not to mention status and even dress, the clerks stood much closer to the employer than to factory labour.'[41]

37

It would be impossible to make such an observation today, at least for the mass of low grade, routine, clerical workers. Advantages which might once have made clerical jobs relatively pleasurable compared with manual labour have been eroded. Offices now tend to be larger and larger, with work stations separated, if at all, by only a few partitions. The benefits of working in city centres, surrounded by shops and amenities, have gradually disappeared. Now, although head offices may still be located in 'desirable' areas, much of the work associated with the particular company has moved to low wage parts of the country or 'greenfield sites' where whole operations—for example processing of credit card transactions—now take place in towns such as Northampton or Southend. The office itself is increasingly dependent on machinery, and the introduction of costly technology changes the whole pace and pattern of work inside the office. Computer technology is able to act as a hidden supervisor both by recording work performed and increasingly by dictating the pace of work. Investment in costly machines leads to the introduction of shift work in order to pay off their cost, with workers on word processors or photocopiers now having to work anti-social hours much more as a matter of course. Clerical work takes on more and more the characteristics of manual labour, with operatives having to learn a number of repetitive tasks in order to service their machines.

Work practices develop alongside this, with the introduction of stricter management controls, more rigidity into the working day and greater emphasis on control from above—whether stricter time controls or performance related pay. The whole change in the work process leads to what has been called the 'proletarianisation' of clerical workers: their becoming more like manual workers in terms of the job and, increasingly, in attitudes.

Certainly in terms of pay, the routine clerical worker is part of the working class. Braverman pointed out over 20 years ago that in the United States, 'the median usual weekly wage for full time clerical work *was lower than that in every type of so called blue collar work.*'[42] Clerical receptionists are some of the lowest paid, with £182 gross weekly earnings (before tax and insurance have been deducted)—a figure which puts them between cleaners and caretakers on the pay scale. Even those in white collar 'professional' jobs such as nurses only had gross earnings of £316 a week. Median gross earnings for 1994 for all women stood at only just over £200 a week.[43] The bulk of female clerical workers are at this figure or below it.

Increasingly, too, white collar workers are becoming proletarianised through joining unions and sometimes even going on strike. One of the dominant features of postwar trade unionism has been the growth of significant white collar trade unions. Today unions such as MSF, Unison and CPSA are as large and organised as their manual counterparts. There were more stoppages last year in public administration and defence, education, health and social work, and community and social services than in any other single industry apart from transport and communication.[44] The largest single union is Unison, with over 1.5 million members, many of them clerical and related workers. A total of 45 percent of professional workers, 43 percent of associate professional and technical, and 27 percent of clerical and secretarial workers were in unions in 1993. This compared with 40 percent of plant and machine operatives being unionised[45] and shows that white collar workers are certainly no less likely to join unions than manual workers.[46]

Skills

One of the most grotesque aspects of capitalism is the way in which it destroys the ability to work and the skills which many workers possess. Craft workers who spent a lifetime learning trades have all but died out, replaced by production processes dependent on the use of machinery, not hand crafted skill.

Here are the words of a leather worker who grained Morocco leather in the Northampton shoe industry:

> The last two years of my working life I earned more money on a secondary job, and I hated every second of it, and I was glad when I took my smock off and retired. I was on a spraying machine that sprayed all kinds of leather, calf and buffalo calf and goat and everything. They eventually had a new machine in from America which would do so many thousands of feet in an hour, where you took a week to do it... My grandfather told me how he used to hand shave the leather; it's now done a hundred times faster by mostly foreign machinery.[47]

His remarks seem to sum up once again the sense that in the past jobs had some worth whereas now they do not. At least in the old days, the argument goes, people did something with their hands which produced a tangible result. But we should be wary of seeing this craft production as representing a golden age of capitalism. The destruction of old skills has been going on as long as capitalism. Even during the 1880s and 1890s in Britain the impact of economic depression and restructuring of industry led to 'the rise of new semi-skilled, machine-operating classes [who] threatened the exclusiveness of the old unions...the gradual change in the industrial pattern for the first time revealed the "semi-skilled" as vital links in the chain of production'.[48]

As capitalism advances it involves a high degree of 'deskilling' of workers. The process described by the leather worker becomes overwhelming as the capitalists invest in new machinery which can do the jobs of sometimes dozens of workers. Mass production techniques mean that the old skills are no longer necessary and no longer worth the investment in wages. Marx writes in *Capital* volume I that:

> It is not the workman that employs the instruments of labour, but the instruments of labour that employ the workman... The separation of the intellectual powers of production from the manual labour, and the conversion of those powers into the might of capital over labour, is...finally completed by modern industry erected on the foundation of machinery. The special skill of each individual insignificant factory operative vanishes as an infinitesimal quantity before the science, the gigantic physical forces, and the mass of labour that are embodied in the factory mechanism and, together with that mechanism, constitute the power of the 'master'.[49]

There was a general tendency for capitalism to deskill as it advanced and techniques once performed by hand could be done by machinery. Machinery also broke down the division of labour between different craft skills which meant jobs once done by several craft workers could now be done by one 'unskilled' or semi-skilled worker. However, it is also worth remembering that many of the craft jobs were not typical of capitalist production, but were restricted, for example, to luxury goods for the rich, with many techniques more akin to pre-capitalist or artisan production.

In addition, as capitalism has acted to break down individual skills, it has also developed new industries which have needed new skills. Indeed it can be argued that as capitalism develops it also raises the general level of skill—literacy, numeracy and so on—in society as a whole. The effect of education inside advanced capitalist societies is to educate the whole working population to a certain level of skill, making them capable of operating complex machinery, understanding written instructions and so on. So whereas the particular level of skill of individual workers diminishes—and a whole number of 'skilled jobs' disappear—the general level of skill inside the mass of the working class rises.

We should also be wary about the whole definition of skilled work with which we are presented. These definitions contain a number of value judgments about what constitutes a skill. So many jobs which are regarded as unskilled today require a degree of learning, training and skill. Jobs such as check out assistants in supermarkets, most forms of clerical work and work in warehouses all require a certain amount of computer literacy, for example. Teaching and nursing are both areas where high degrees of skill are required even though these are not the sorts of skills needed for toolmaking. And work in high street printing shops is not fundamentally different from much ordinary printing. One woman employed in such work described it like this:

> I saw an ad for a part time photocopy operator. It's supposed to be like working in a shop, but in fact it couldn't be more different. It's more than being a shop assistant. You have to be numerate, and quick, and able to talk to customers about printing and what their requirements are.[50]

Skilled work often led to the most narrow and sectional form of workplace organisation. While it is true that sometimes skilled workers built movements which challenged the system, for example during the struggles of engineering workers in Sheffield and Glasgow during the First World War, the skilled workers of the late 19th century quite often saw their unions as excluding other workers.[51] Even in modern times, the divisions in areas such as print working between 'skilled' and 'unskilled' severely weakened the various trade unions to the benefit of the employers. A chapel secretary (workplace branch representative) of the print union SOGAT at the Bemrose plant on Merseyside describes the situation in the early 1980s, where the skilled union NGA members saw preserving the wage differential as the most important thing:

> The NGA fella would be on about £12,000 and the SLADE

fella would be on about £16,000, but the NGA fella was happy because he was earning more than the SOGAT fella. Those bigots would sooner keep *your* wages down than see you fighting management.[52]

The idea that skilled work is a thing of the past also rests on a faulty assessment of what were skilled jobs. So miners and dockers are usually included as being 'skilled' workers even though these jobs have generally been classified as unskilled. The main reason for this is a confusion that 'skilled' equals 'well organised' workers, in the same way that manual workers are deemed to be more militant than white collar workers. It is true that many workers today are less well organised than dockers or miners have been in some past periods, though by no means always. But the organisation of dockers and miners did not arise primarily from a monopoly of skills which other workers did not possess. Rather it came from a series of struggles which organised these workers in such a way that their bargaining position was strengthened.

Incomes and lifestyles

Perhaps the most pervasive argument about the decline of the working class is that whatever the objective status of white collar workers, their incomes and lifestyles are such that they tend not to see themselves as workers. Workers are bought off to such an extent that the majority of them become effectively part of the middle class, leaving a less fortunate 'underclass' living on benefits and missing out on the consumer society which the rest of us have embraced so readily.

However, a more common experience for the large majority of the population is of debt, insecurity and poverty. Wages for the vast majority are low: the incomes of the bottom 50 percent of the population are all under £200 a week. Only 1.3 million individuals have an income of over £700 a week, and only the top 10 percent of the population receive over £400 a week.[53] One book on class puts it that 'at most, one in five employees earns more than £20,000 a year—and that is before tax... Four in ten—a total approaching 10 million people—take home between £10,000 and £20,000; nearly six in ten take home between £7,500 and £20,000.'[54] This hardly suggests the two thirds prosperous, one third deprived, society which we are often told—not least by the

Labour leaders—is the make up of the British population. Rather the picture is one of a minority of people who are very comfortably off, and perhaps four fifths who are insecure, worried about money, and who find a larger and larger proportion of their income being spent on paying for pension plans and the like to ensure they can stay above the poverty line in old age.

The income of the vast majority also gives the lie to the idea that society is polarised between the very rich on the one hand and a dispossessed underclass on the other with a mass of contented 'middle class' in between. The very rich are certainly there. But the very poor are themselves very often part of the working class. There is not a big gap between the 'well off' and the 'poor' working class—indeed they often belong to the same families or social class. One reason for much working class sympathy for the unemployed or pensioners is that most workers understand how precarious their incomes are and how quickly they can fall from one group to the other.

It is this feeling of insecurity which explains attitudes over benefits which are much more liberal than the average *Sun* editorial or speech at the Tory party conference would have us believe. A 1993 survey showed that 55 percent agreed that 'people receiving social security are made to feel like second class citizens', whereas 22 percent disagreed; 53 percent thought 'the government should spend more on welfare benefits for the poor even if it leads to higher taxes', while 20 percent disagreed; while only 25 percent agreed that 'if welfare benefits weren't so generous, people would learn to stand on their own two feet', with 52 percent against.[55]

Is there an underclass?

A vivid picture of society is conjured up by talk of an underclass. It is a society where supposedly the contented majority are becoming better off, but feel their lives threatened by a growing band of people both within the same society, but also outside it. While the majority live in pleasant suburbs, invest much time and money in the quality of their own and their children's lives, and have access to prosperity through their hard work and endeavours, the minority are governed by different motivations.[56]

They live in run down council estates, and are either long term unemployed or living on benefits. Their children are the

43

'failures' of the education system, leaving school only to join the army of the unskilled who themselves either suffer frequent un-employment or have access to low wage jobs. Many of them turn to crime as an alternative and so the estates also become centres of joy riding, burglary and 'mugging'.

The fear of the underclass is such that it now pervades the newspapers, radio and television, films. Increasingly, and espe-cially in the US, houses and flats with security doors and fences, or even security guards and private police forces are deemed nec-essary to keep out the hordes of 'have-nots' and protect the lifestyles of the 'haves'. One view of this social polarisation was put by a financial journalist:

> In time, our form of capitalism will come to resemble the American variety. We will not regard ourselves as part of a society, but merely as individuals who must fend for ourselves as best we may, and devil take the hindmost.
>
> With even more of the poor always with us, we will not seek to provide security as a public good; we will buy burglar and car alarms, anti-theft radios, private picket gates. We will earn more and spend more just to maintain the same sense of security we had when society was kinder and fairer. We will drive from a night-watchman-protected dormitory through ghettoes of the underclass to security-coded office buildings. Shut out the world, we want to be rich—whatever the cost.[57]

Before looking at whether an underclass exists in reality rather than in the fevered imagination of journalists and advertising copywriters, it is worth a brief consideration of the politics behind the concept. First there is an eerie echo from the past: the underclass arguments could come directly from the Victorian middle classes. They too feared the 'people of the abyss', fled the slum areas of cities and regarded large sections of the poor as barely human. Most importantly, they believed that the poor were poor because they were too lazy or stupid or in some other way at fault to be otherwise. These people had to be forced to work by society in order to redeem themselves. This was the philosophy behind the Poor Law which led to the 19th century workhouses. In the US poorhouses, even where no profitable work was avail-able, inmates still had to work 'at something which is not prof-itable, at all events they must be kept employed', and an observer had seen 'a party of men, carrying wood from one corner of the yard to another and piling it there; when it was all removed it was brought back and piled in the old place.'[58]

Listening to Newt Gingrich in the US railing against 'criminals' or John Redwood in Britain attacking single mothers on benefit it is hard to see any difference of substance between them and their ancestors who distinguished between the 'deserving' and 'undeserving' poor. '"Underclass" in radical-right usage designates a segment of the population whose lifestyle, of indiscipline, is dangerous; whose precise numbers are less important than the contagious spread of their example; and whose material poverty, in so far as acknowledged, is self-induced.'[59]

The underclass suffer because supposedly they refuse to spend their money wisely—instead it goes on drink, lottery tickets, cigarettes and videos. They have little money in the first place either because they refuse to work at all or because they wilfully fail to take advantage of the education system and so gain few or no qualifications which would get them work. Even worse, they insist on having children often outside marriage and are therefore plunged further into poverty.

These ideas permeate the far right and form one of the basic planks of their politics. For them, the problem lies not in the market system but in individuals. However, these views have an echo among sections of liberal and even supposedly left wing opinion. They start from a higher degree of compassion but also tend to blame the victims of society rather than those who have caused their poverty and misery in the first place. Tony Blair's New Labour leadership, for example, has taken to referring to the working class as 'the unskilled' and accepts that crime, poverty and joblessness are all at least in part individual problems—not part of a wider social crisis. Particularly feared by some on the left are young men: many face unemployment, they are the group most likely to be involved in crime (although usually against each other) and are also those most likely to be excluded from schools, truant and so on. Some writers see young men as one of the greatest social problems because unemployment is a threat to their masculinity.

The fear, dislike and ignorance of many underclass theories suggest that they have less to do with rational discussion than with blind prejudice. In the case of the right wing theories, there is also a strong element of racism since the inner city ghettoes, problems of single parents and so on are explicitly seen as involving disproportionate numbers of blacks.

None of this should hide the fact that essentially what is being talked about as an underclass in these theories is a very substantial section of the working class: workers who have fallen into unemployment or homelessness, but also many who do not fit into this category. Age, motherhood, tenancy of council flats, a criminal record and even just simply low wages are enough to push millions towards 'underclass' status. As J K Galbraith has pointed out, the supposed 'underclass' is composed largely of people who work in essential but poorly paid jobs. 'The underclass is integrally a part of a larger economic process, and…serves the living standard and the comfort of the more favoured community.'[60]

The numbers of people falling into 'underclass' categories are much more than a tiny minority. Low earners compose the biggest single group of the poor. Nearly four in every ten adults working full time in 1994 were earning less than the Council of Europe's 'decency threshold' of £221.50 gross per week.[61]

Of those classified as poor in Britain—a total of 13.9 million people—a full 4.6 million have an income from employment. Even when the self employed are excluded, 3.2 million have an income from work. Another 3.6 million are aged over 60 and 2.8 million are unemployed.[62]

The largest groups of the poor are therefore either people working at present—and consequently part of the working class—or pensioners and unemployed workers. Unless we are to believe that becoming older leads people to change the class to which they belong, then we have to accept that pensioners are workers who can no longer work and so are surplus to the requirements of the capitalists.

The same is true of the bulk of the unemployed, and indeed others living on benefits. Most single mothers, many unemployed and even some people on sickness benefit will return to the workforce at some time in the future, but at any one time find themselves outside the workforce for a variety of reasons. They will live in the same streets, be part of the same families, and their children will go to the same schools as employed workers.

They are part of the reserves of labour which are so important to the capitalist class. When Karl Marx discussed the 19th century equivalents of the 'underclass' he pointed to various sorts of reserves: the floating, the latent and the stagnant. The floating were those such as casual or seasonal workers who went in and out of employment in areas like building or agriculture. Similar workers obviously still exist, although their numbers as a total of the workforce are not very significant. Latent reserves are those who are drawn into paid work on a permanent basis—rural workers who move to the cities, women who leave the home to take up work. Stagnant reserves are those most akin to an underclass: long term unemployed who work only intermittently. In addition there are those on the fringes of employment or those who live by crime.[63]

Clearly, there are groups of such people within capitalist society today, but they do not constitute a class by any description. There are substantial numbers of homeless. Shelter believes that the 'unofficial homeless' could be as high as 1.7 million, with 8,000 sleeping rough. Local authorities accepted as homeless 420,000 people in 1991.[64] Once homeless, it is notoriously difficult to obtain regular work and to hang on to it, hence the high proportion of homeless with no income and access only to the most casual work.

But people do not choose to be homeless: homelessness is a result of the market and government policies which cut benefit to young people living at home, refuse to build cheap public housing and preside over a low wage economy where it often seems pointless to work. Nor are they from an 'underclass'—one in ten residents in St Mungo hotels and care homes have a degree.[65] Another study showed that 86 percent of young homeless left home involuntarily because of factors such as abuse or family breakdown.[66] The same is true for the unemployed: most unemployed want to work, and most young unemployed do in fact gain paid work. The biggest number of long term unemployed is older men: in 1993, 'over 53 percent of men aged 50 to 64 were unemployed for more than a year, compared with only 26 percent of those aged 16 to 19.'[67] Whereas young men have the highest short term unemployment rates, this is reversed after one year, suggesting that many do find work.

Being on the receiving end of benefits, very poor or outside work is therefore often a transitory phase. Most of those young people who at present are of such concern to underclass theorists will not stay in that position: they will get work, go to college, return to work when their children are at school. Even pensioners are returning to the workforce in greater numbers—on a part time basis usually—to supplement their miserable state pension.

The 'underclass' are the same as the rest of us in most senses—except they tend to be among the poorest. But even in this, they will be closer to nearly every worker than employed workers are to the middle or ruling classes. Nor is it necessarily a permanent state. A study of 'disadvantaged' families found that only a third of children and families classified as multiply disadvantaged at age 11 were still so at 16, and half of those multiply disadvantaged at 16 had not been at 11. Other studies show considerable discontinuity as well as continuity of social disadvantage; and that those long term unemployed or on benefits had the same attitudes as everyone else.[68] Or as a report of the Rowntree Foundation study *Life on a Low Income* put it: 'the poor are not an underclass. According to [the] study...they are people who want to work, want a decent home, and yearn for an income that will pay their bills.'[69]

It is society which has pushed some of these people to the margins—by denying them work and ensuring that because of this their income level is at the poorest; by denying them a minimum wage which could take their earnings out of poverty levels; and by denying them access to affordable housing, decent education or health care. The attempts to scapegoat such people will continue as long as the capitalists try to blame working people for the crisis. While some working class people fall for these arguments, the facts of working class life cut across them. Most families have members or friends who are unemployed, live on benefits and have older members who cannot survive on their pension. Indeed, many would be destitute without family support. Most know the fears of insecurity, of losing jobs or houses.

There is no wall between the two different sorts of people. Those who are unemployed want their children to be able to work. A woman who cleans offices two hours a day will still prefer her children to obtain qualifications so they can work full time. Workers living on housing estates—and council rented accommodation still makes up 5 million dwellings[70]—want their children to stay out of trouble with the police, but find this increasingly difficult when they are poor.

The underclass theories fulfil an important political role, however—of trying to divide workers between the employed and unemployed, the 'respectable' and the 'disreputable', the 'thrifty' and the 'feckless'. The people who gain from this are what the sociologist Peter Townsend calls the 'overclass'—those who have gained most from society and who can only benefit from turning workers against each other.[71]

As this chapter has shown, far from the working class being dead, or dying, the actual situation of the mass of working people is that they are forced to sell their labour power for a wage that covers their subsistence but little else, and that they face an exploiting class which has done its utmost over the past two decades to squeeze more and more profit from working people—whether through cuts in the 'social wage' or through raising the level of productivity. No wonder that a recent Gallup poll showed that 81 percent of people in Britain believe there is a class struggle, compared with 66 percent 15 years ago.[72] So how is it that our rulers hang on to their rule, and why do workers not do more to gain what is theirs? It is to these questions that we now turn.

Born to rule

The capitalist class is by definition a tiny class compared with society as a whole. But it is a class apart. Its monopoly of wealth and power ensures that it has access to a lifestyle quite distinct and removed from any other class.

Extraordinary privilege is concentrated in a very small group. They have wealth; and the near total security in life, the latitude of choice, the ease in everyday management and manipulation of people and things around them, which all go with wealth. They have power: less because they actively direct affairs—though many of them do that—than because the anonymous regulation of affairs by principles of property, profit and market is in tune with their interests. And they are well placed to pass on their privileges to their children. The core of this group is those who own and those who control capital on a large scale.[1]

This tiny group of people—one estimate puts it at no more than one or two per thousand head of population—are by any definition the wealthiest, the most powerful, and the most certain that their unequal position is justified. The inequality is not in doubt. The top 1 percent of the population own around a fifth of all marketable wealth and the richest 5 percent have at least as big a share of income between them as the whole of the poorest one third.[2]

Their ownership and control of capital mean that the interest of the capitalist class lies in exploiting workers. The capitalists live off the surplus value that they extract from workers, and so are driven to hostility to the working class—to cutting their wages, lengthening the working day, making them pay more for welfare. It is irrelevant whether an individual capitalist has a humane or paternalist attitude, or whether they follow this path aggressively—the drive to capital accumulation and the competition between the different capitalists ensures that they try to organise exploitation in the most efficient way possible to suit their needs.

Being a capitalist today is about more than just ownership of wealth. Frederick Engels, adding a note to *The Communist Manifesto* in 1888, defined the capitalist class as follows: 'by bourgeoisie is meant the class of modern capitalists, owners of the means of social production and employers of wage labour'.[3] This remains the best definition. But the stereotypical picture of the northern capitalist, owner of one or two factories or mills who employs few managers and who is closely involved in the direct exploitation of workers, is more suited to the 1840s than to the 1990s.

Today world capitalism is dominated by a relatively small number of huge companies, often multinational, which are directly owned by shareholders but whose day to day running is in the hands of individuals appointed and paid vast salaries to run them efficiently. Every major capitalist state intervenes directly in the running of capitalism, sometimes through nationalised industries, sometimes through subsidies or investment in infrastructure such as railways. The top salaried bosses of these enterprises are just as much part of the capitalist class if we accept a definition which includes both ownership and control of capital. Ownership of the means of production (the factories and so on) applies to some capitalists, but there are as many who manage and control enterprises which they do not actually own (although they will probably own substantial shares in the company). So any definition has to include those who both own and control capital and who through their ownership or control of the means of production are able to exploit workers.

These professional 'controllers of capital' have become more important to capitalism as it has developed, requiring more sophisticated means of extracting surplus value from workers. Ownership of capital itself—especially inherited ownership—does   51 not necessarily make the individual a dynamic and efficient capitalist. He or she may be more used to and better at spending money than at running a company. Therefore the capitalist class draws on resources from within its own class and a few from outside its ranks in order to organise itself:

> To belong to the capitalist class by virtue of ownership of capital, one must simply possess adequate wealth; that is the only requirement for membership in that sense. To belong to the capitalist class in its aspect as the direct organiser and manager of a capitalist enterprise is another matter. Here, a process of selection goes on having to do with such qualities as aggressiveness and ruthlessness, organisational proficiency and drive, technical insight, and especially marketing talent.
>
> Thus while the managerial stratum continues to be drawn from among those endowed with capital, family, connections, and other ties within the network of the class as a whole, it is not closed to some who may rise from other social classes, not through the acquisition of wealth on their part but through the co-optation of their talent on the part of the capitalist organisation which they serve. In this case the ownership of capital later follows from the managerial position, rather than the other way around.[4]

These top managers and employers are in every essential the same as the capitalists and cannot be seen—as middle managers might be—as simply the servants of the capitalists. They organise the system and share in its spoils. 'Directors and senior managers cannot in real terms be seen as deriving their salaries and other rewards primarily from the sale of their labour in the market. They are able in large part to determine their own remuneration …because they occupy positions of control. Their rewards…are a claim on profits.'[5] The salaried employers may appear to shade into a burgeoning middle class but are very different from their lower counterparts by reason of wealth, power, decision making abilities and consequent social standing. 'Their formal attribute of being part of the same payroll as the production workers, clerk, and porters of the corporation no more robs them of the powers of decision and command over the others in the enterprise than does the fact that the general, like the private, wears the military uniform, or the pope and the cardinal pronounce the same liturgy as the parish priest.'[6]

What is true for those directly involved in controlling capitalist enterprises is also true for the elites in various areas which surround them. The capitalist class can, through its ownership and control of wealth, ensure that within its ranks are the 'opinion formers' such as national newspaper editors and top television producers, the top QCs and judges, those appointed to positions such as the governor of the Bank of England, the vice-chancellors of colleges and the like. These, their families and associates comprise the capitalist or ruling class—or at least part of it.

Being a capitalist cannot simply be classified as owning wealth but has to also include the control and running of enterprises, nor can it simply be defined by who runs industry, the banks and other forms of big business. The government itself, the state structure of police and army, the judiciary and the civil service are all institutions run on behalf of and for the benefit of the capitalist class. Very substantial numbers of the people who run these institutions have been through the public school and Oxbridge systems. In 1992 an *Economist* survey of 100 'top people' found that nearly all were male, and that over half had gone to Oxbridge and two thirds to public school. In the same year, biographies of almost 1,000 civil servants revealed that more than half were Oxbridge educated and that eight of the 12 biggest government departments were run by public school and Oxbridge graduates.[7]

As the system has developed and aged, so the state has taken on a bigger and bigger role which has been twofold. Firstly it acts to protect the capitalist class and the capitalists' wealth from those they exploit; secondly it tries to organise capitalist production in the most efficient way possible. The state is a recognition that the free market alone does not operate necessarily in the collective interest of the capitalist class. Moreover, state ownership is itself a result of competition, as failing or weak capitals are nationalised or given injections of government cash in order to enable them to compete internationally.

So during the 19th century the bulk of the capitalist class embarked on a series of measures involving the state which would ensure a healthier and more productive workforce: sanitary measures, better housing, laws preventing the worst outrages of the early factory system. The tendency to nationalisation and greater state control of industry was already in evidence, especially in areas such as the railways and postal communications where the state needed to intervene in order to ensure efficient communication. The state came to represent capital as a whole, as opposed to the individual—sometimes partial and sometimes conflicting—interests of separate capitals.[8]

In the 1870s Frederick Engels pointed to the increasing role of state finance in pushing capitalist development in a certain direction and wrote:

> The modern state, no matter what its form, is essentially a capitalist machine, the state of the capitalists, the ideal personification of the total national capital.[9]

As competition between capitalists took on the form of competition between rival nation states and empires—as it did in the age of imperialism at the end of the 19th century—so the role of the capitalist state became more important in directing various capitals and bringing other sections of capital directly under its control.

If the state represents the interests of the capitalist class collectively then the whole apparatus of the state at its senior levels can only be understood as part of the capitalist class. The judges, top civil servants, heads of government agencies and quangos, may not directly organise the exploitation of workers in the sense of running businesses, but they play an important role in ensuring the process of exploitation is a smooth one. There are many direct connections between the capitalists themselves and their counterparts within the state and government. Connections of family and education are obvious. But the cohesion of the ruling class does not depend directly on ties of family; rather it rests on more informal ideas and connections:

> The strength of business is manifest in its ties with a variety of other influential groups and bodies: directly with the Conservative Party, the commercial press and a range of pressure groups; less directly but none the less effectively with the machinery of state and the broadcasting media. These links are formed in part as bonds of common experience among top people. But the power of the ruling interest is found in the set of common assumptions which govern the routine workings of the economy, government and mass communications. Those assumptions—the core assumptions of the society—indicate the central place of business, because they are business assumptions: principles of property, profit and market dominance in the running of affairs.[10]

The sense in which this class is cohesive and organised and pushing in the same direction can be seen from the way that direct political involvement is quite often secondary to it. The Tory party is the favoured party of the vast majority of the ruling class, because it is openly pro big business and seeks to make life as easy as possible for the capitalists. But, with a few exceptions, the people who run big business or any of the institutions of the state tend to take a back seat when it comes to political activity. Professional politicians—especially in the Tory party but also increasingly inside the Labour Party—tend to be drawn from the professional groups such as lawyers rather than from the ruling class itself. These people may become members of the ruling class by dint of their wealth, position and power, but they do not necessarily start off that way. So Margaret Thatcher, herself from a lower middle class background of small shopkeepers, has managed through a combination of marriage, amassing her own personal wealth and a position of political power to become part of the ruling class. The advantage to the ruling class of recruiting their 'officers' from such backgrounds is that they have the advantage of being nearer to the mass of people and are therefore able to pose as ordinary housewives, men of the people and so on.

The divisions inside the capitalist class are very real. There is direct competition between capitalists—for example, between the soap powder manufacturers Lever Brothers and Procter & Gamble, or between the bosses of Eurotunnel and those who own the cross Channel ferries. There are conflicts of interest between that section of the capitalist class which looks to Europe for its markets and those who look to the US or to the 'Asian tiger' economies. There are differences in tactics, as when some employers prefer to use the anti-union laws, while others would rather avoid direct confrontation. These divisions reflect a system based on competition between different capitals. Rupert Murdoch will be happy if he is making money at the expense of Lord Rothermere's papers, and his ultimate aim will be to dominate a market with perhaps four daily papers, each of which is controlled by him. But he will also be united with Lord Rothermere in the common aim of squeezing as much surplus value out of their own particular workers and out of the working class in general (through higher taxation and less public spending for example).

None of these divisions are fundamental—although they can be decisive when they produce major crises inside the ruling class and when the working class is relatively united in fighting against them. Nonetheless the capitalist class has a common interest in exploiting the working class, and in hanging on to as much of the profits which it extracts from the surplus value of workers as it possibly can:

> In each particular sphere of production the individual capitalist, as well as the capitalists as a whole, take direct part in the exploitation of the total working class by the totality of capital and in the degree of that exploitation, not only out of general class sympathy, but also for direct economic reasons. For, assuming all other conditions...to be given, the average rate of profit depends on the intensity of exploitation of the sum total of labour by the sum total of capital.[11]

In periods of expansion and boom, the capitalists are content enough to allow some crumbs from their table to fall to the workers they exploit. But the crisis prone nature of the system means that such gains can never be guaranteed. Economic crisis deepens the competition between capitals and leads the various capitalists to attempt to increase the surplus value which they extract from their workers in order to fend off competition from their rivals.

The crisis also leads the capitalist states to cut back on benefits such as welfare, health and education as a means of further squeezing more out of workers to the advantage of capital in general:

> As soon as it no longer is a question of sharing profits, but of sharing losses, everyone tries to reduce his own share to a minimum and to shove it off upon another. The class, as such, must inevitably lose. How much the individual capitalist must bear of the loss, ie, to what extent he must share in it at all, is decided by strength and cunning, and competition then becomes a fight among hostile brothers.[12]

But their position as hostile brothers does not override the fact that they are brothers—rivals, but with similar interests in terms of exploitation.

This class cohesion is one reason why the capitalist class hangs on to its rule. It is the class which is the most developed materially and which has access not only to the wealth of society, but to a range of ideas and social institutions which enhance its own belief in its duty and ability to rule. Its wealth is fabulous, and while wealth alone cannot be the means of deciding who is in a particular class, it is possible to tell quite a lot about who the capitalists are by how they live. The five top richest in terms of personal wealth according to one survey are Paul Raymond (pornography), David Sainsbury (supermarkets), Lord Rothermere (newspapers), Sir Evelyn Rothschild (banking) and the Duke of Westminster (landowning).[13]

Their personal wealth ranges from £1,650 million for Raymond to a mere £900 million for the Duke of Westminster. Nearly all the surveys of wealth underestimate actual wealth possessed by the rich, who ensure that their accountants and lawyers use the maximum number of schemes for tax avoidance and the like.

The capitalist class is highly insular. One of the greatest myths of capitalist society is that anyone can make it if only they have enough drive and are willing to work hard enough. We are constantly told of entrepreneurs such as Richard Branson who have come from nothing to make millions. But these people usually come from a background of some wealth (Branson and Michael Heseltine, for example, both came from prosperous backgrounds and went to public school). While the common myth is that the capitalists are 'risk takers' and entrepreneurs, such people make up only a small minority of the most wealthy, most of whom gain their money through inheritance and being born with privilege and advantage in the first place.

Whole families recur again and again among the richest—the Rothschild family of bankers, the Guinnesses, who made a fortune from brewing, and the Moores family who own Littlewoods Pools. The fact that even the younger members of these dynasties are among some of the wealthiest people in Britain is a sign of the way in which capitalist wealth is kept within the bounds of a relatively small number of families.

Wealth is retained through the generations. This is obviously true of those from aristocratic backgrounds, such as the Duke of Westminster, but it is also true of more recently wealthy families. The only reason why members of the Moores family, or the young Guinnesses, are able to amass millions of pounds worth of wealth by the time they are just past adolescence is because they inherit it. A study of men who died in the late 1950s leaving estates of over £100,000 showed that half of them had 'inherited at least £50,000 from his father. Two in every three had inherited at least £10,000.'[14]

The capitalist class has extensive ties of kinship which ensure that it passes on its privilege and wealth. While the kinship ties of working class people can be a buffer against insecurity, those of the ruling class are about creating a cocoon of privilege which enables those already born with advantages in life to make the most of them.[15]

Ensuring that this control is maintained and passed from one generation of our rulers to another is no simple task. It requires an elaborate and detailed structure which ensures that from an early age the ruling class learns how to rule.

Public schools like Eton, Winchester and Harrow instil into their privileged pupils the sense that they are superior to the rest of us and that they are 'natural leaders' whose place in society is firmly at the top. The children of the ruling class are sent to boarding schools from the age of seven, and are cut off from ordinary people of any description apart from those who are there to serve them.

These schools are the fast track to the elite universities of Oxford and Cambridge, which still supply a very high proportion of those who staff the capitalist state, government and the boardrooms of big business. There the children of the ruling class—plus a handful of outsiders who are considered bright enough to be allowed into the charmed circle—mix with their contemporaries who will one day run the key capitalist institutions.

Every area of life is covered by the same exclusive gatherings. Meeting places of the wealthy in the months of May, June and July include the Chelsea Flower Show, cricket test matches, the Derby and Royal Ascot, Glyndebourne opera, Wimbledon, Henley and gold cup polo.[16] This summer season of race meetings and regattas sees our rulers gathering socially to arrange connections, marriages and, most importantly, develop informal business links. The rich live in their own exclusive areas such as Mayfair, Belgravia and Knightsbridge where they patronise street after street of elite shops and restaurants. Some male members of the capitalist class attend exclusive West End gentlemen's clubs where they socialise and discuss politics, business and the problems of ruling. They frequent the ballet, opera, theatre and classical music concerts not so much for entertainment as for the social prestige and contacts which these places attract. Even their religion—the Anglican church—is dominated by the middle and upper classes. And of course the capitalist class has its own party, the Tory party, which virtually every major capitalist supports.

These institutions are a means of educating their own members, of instilling into them a sense of class consciousness and cohesion, and of drawing into their orbit those who were born outside the ruling class but who by dint of wealth or position can now become part of it. So the small number of self made businessmen learn quickly that the best way into the capitalist elite is ensuring that their children go to the same schools and marry into this class.

There are bonds of intermarriage and inter-investment between different sections of the capitalist class. Even as capitalism was developing in Britain, the old aristocracy—which no longer wielded independent, decisive economic and political control—tended to preserve its status and landed wealth by marrying into the emerging capitalist class and so gaining access to new found sources of riches. Today the aristocracy is regarded by many as an anachronism, a sign that British society has never really modernised and that much power still lies with the monarchy, House of Lords and other trappings of medieval society. This is to mistake the extent to which the remains of the British aristocracy have become integrated into capitalist society both by marriage within the capitalist class and—more importantly—by themselves becoming capitalists. By the 18th century aristocrats such as the Duke of Argyll were developing into capitalist oligarchs making money in iron, coal and salt. Many of the mineowners—such as Lord Londonderry—began as aristocratic landowners. As capitalism developed, so the division between aristocrats and capitalists diminished. Today the aristocracy is not separate from but an integral part of the capitalist class, both often as big players within the capitalist system, and also through playing an important role in providing a sense of continuity and tradition within British society.

It is often argued that there is a deep cleavage between financial and manufacturing capital—that the money men in the City hold industrialists to ransom. This has been used to justify alliances between workers and sections of the industrial capitalists against 'international capital'. Since the rise of the City and the deregulation of financial markets in the 1980s, this argument has taken on renewed force. Finance capital moves freely and has no particular ties to Britain or indeed to Europe. But the increasing internationalisation of capital means that this multinational character is true of much industrial capital as well. And as capitalism has become more international so the links between industrial and financial capital have become stronger. Some industrial companies now have their own financial operations, and finance capital has become key to the large number of industrial mergers. Inter-investment now means that many companies contain elements of both under the same umbrella, while finance capital is a means of smoothing the path of much manufacturing capital and is not in direct competition with it.

Again, there is no real difference between the public sector capitalists and those in the private sector—witness the ease with which the heads of the public utilities moved over to be heads of the private utilities, at triple the salary.

The capitalists' consciousness as a class is acute. They understand that they are the immensely rich and powerful rulers of a society fashioned for their benefit. This class consciousness only goes so far, because the individual capitalist is incapable of seeing beyond his own particular position to an accurate picture of society as a whole. As Franz Jakubowski has written:

> The means of production are produced socially and for society, but are in the hands of individual capitalists. 'Capitalism is not a personal but a social power', but the movements of this power are directed by the owners of capital, who do not have an overall view of the social role of their activity... Private ownership of the means of production means that the only possible view from the position of the bourgeoisie is that of the individual capitalist.[17]

And while the 'bourgeoisie is as much subject to self-alienation as the proletariat...unlike the proletariat, the bourgeoisie has no interest in seeing through and beyond this self-alienation or in removing it.'[18]

But the bourgeoisie could not hang on to its wealth without at least the partial acquiescence of the working class—the fact that workers' alienation leaves them feeling powerless to do anything to affect their lives, and that they can only overcome this alienation in the process of changing the world. Insofar as much of the time most workers feel that they can do little to change their circumstances, the capitalist class is able to continue its rule by consent more frequently than by direct force. This allows it to maintain its monopoly of wealth and power, which in turn help it to reinforce its position. The intermediate layers inside society perform a crucial role in all this. At the top, those closest in lifestyle and power to the capitalist class (sometimes called the 'upper middle classes') are central to cementing their power—ideologically through television and newspapers, in key managerial roles, as the top professional doctors and lawyers, as MPs. These people tend to be both the loyal lieutenants of capital and a transmission belt in ensuring that their ideas and wishes are carried in wider society.

Ideological identification with the system is very important as a means of keeping the 'middle layers' of society committed to it. But the economic uncertainties many of these people now face make them begin to challenge some of the accepted ideas. To understand how we need to look in some detail at the 'middle class'.

Caught in the middle?

'I can tell you, I'm pretty middle class'. When Labour's deputy leader John Prescott made this statement on the BBC radio *Today* programme in April 1996 his remarks were greeted with a mixture of shock and disdain. How could a man who left secondary modern school at 15, became a merchant navy steward and union activist and who still talks with a northern accent be anything but working class? Yet Prescott was only expressing the fact that his MP's salary, his two homes and his position as a leading shadow cabinet politician put him outside of the working class in most respects apart from his origins.

His remarks were welcomed by those who want to pretend that 'we are all middle class now'. To them, class is an outdated concept which fitted an old England of aristocrats and cloth caps, but has no place now. The columnist Tony Parsons wrote in the *Daily Mirror* of Prescott's class position:

> When the traditional manufacturing industries disappeared, so did the traditional working class. Jobs and entire communities were consigned to history. There are now more university lecturers than coal miners in Britain.

He continued: 'Now the middle class is by far the broadest stratum in society. It covers suburb, city and country. It takes in the shopkeeper, the self employed builder and, of course, the Labour politician.'[1]

Shopkeepers, self employed builders and Labour politicians of course only cover a tiny number of the population and therefore could not possibly be said to represent 'the broadest stratum of society.' But Parsons' statements reflect more than a simple misunderstanding of who is working class. The changing structure of society in recent decades has also given rise to a number of misapprehensions about what is 'middle class'.

Throughout the 20th century, but especially since 1945 in the advanced capitalist countries there has been a huge expansion in the number of jobs which are designated professional or managerial. These jobs usually require higher education qualifications, are salaried and usually receive considerably higher remuneration and much greater 'status' than the more 'traditional' working class jobs.

The expansion of this work has been in three areas: in the number of managers at every level; the number of what are sometimes called 'headfixers'—those whose role is to help sort out capitalism's problems and carry its ideas, such as social workers, teachers, lecturers and the like; and in the number of professionals needed to run advanced capitalist society, for example doctors, lawyers and architects. This last group has always existed, but now they tend to be organised in bigger workplaces, often as salaried employees working for large law or architecture firms.

Perhaps the initial point to make is that many of those who are considered 'middle class' should by any serious definition be regarded as part of the working class. This is true for the great army of technicians who perform skilled white collar jobs whose wages, conditions of work, lack of control over the work process and training all bring characteristics virtually identical to traditional workers to their jobs. They 'have very little autonomy in their labour; exercise no supervisory role, add value to the production of goods and services; come from traditional working class backgrounds; receive an income and maintain a lifestyle comparable to that of the working class'.[2] These workers—draughtsmen, lab technicians, computer operators, air traffic controllers—are in many instances directly productive of surplus value for their employers in exactly the same way as are, say,

63

workers in a car factory.

Then there is another group who are clearly not directly producing profits for the capitalists and not producing commodities. This includes teachers, social workers, health workers of various descriptions, and many more involved in state employment and who certainly in popular imagery are considered 'middle class' or professional. Yet they are in most respects identical to the workers mentioned above in terms of income, lifestyles or background. The role in society of some, like teachers, will be, it is true, at least partly to transmit the ruling ideas in society to the whole of the working class. But at least equally as important is the role of teachers and nurses and similar workers in the job of ensuring that the next generation of workers is educated, literate and healthy. In this sense their jobs, as part of the developed state system essential to the advanced capitalist countries, are essential to the reproduction of labour power and therefore contribute indirectly to the production of surplus value.

These various groups of workers now make up substantial sectors of the working class. At the other end of the spectrum it is also fairly easy to identify those who are clearly structured in to the running of capitalist society on behalf of the capitalist class. If we take into account college principals, heads of the biggest schools, top architects, QCs, medical consultants, the higher ranks in the armed forces, columnists on national newspapers and so on—as well as the higher echelons of management in private industry, and top civil servants and local government heads of department—then it is clear that they are there to ensure the smooth running of the system and usually this is true in terms of their identification with the system and their rewards in terms of a substantial share of the collective surplus value produced.

However, between these two groups (and even here there is a degree of overlap) it is much harder to draw sharp distinctions. Harry Braverman has written about managers in private industry:

> Since the authority and expertise of the middle ranks in the capitalist corporation represent an unavoidable delegation of responsibility, the position of such functionaries may best be judged by their relation to the power and wealth that commands them from above, and to the mass of labour beneath them which they in turn help to control, command, and organise. Their pay level is significant because beyond a certain

point it, like the pay of the commanders of the corporation, clearly represents not just the exchange of their labour power for money—a commodity exchange—but a *share in the surplus* produced in the corporation, and thus is intended to attach them to the success or failure of the corporation and give them a 'management stake' even if a small one.[3]

The same could equally apply to a whole number of managerial and professional positions which may not be directly concerned with supervision and control over the work process of others but where employees find themselves in a position of trust for capital or where they occupy semi-autonomous positions where they can to a certain extent set their own agendas: university lecturers, higher ranking journalists, lawyers might—although do not necessarily—fall into this category.

These groups are not qualitatively different from the old 'hangers on' of the capitalist class which Marx saw as identifying with the ruling class. Their salaries and various benefits—company cars, private health insurance, pension plans and the like—indicate that the majority of them are not exploited and instead identify with the system. Far from producing surplus value, they are paid out of the collective surplus value of others and therefore tend to take a (albeit very small) share of the capitalist cake.

However, even here the lines can be blurred. For example it is possible to regard lecturers in FE colleges (apart from the highest grades which are often structurally part of management) as a modern form of what used to be known as the 'aristocracy of labour': essentially within the working class, indirectly productive of surplus value since their job is to impart fairly basic skills to young workers, paid slightly higher wages and working under more preferable and less routinised conditions than factory workers or routine clerical workers. As we shall see below, the conditions of work for this group have deteriorated considerably in recent years making them closer to other groups of workers in wages, conditions and consciousness.

But what about, say, the head teacher of a primary school? At one level such posts are part of a professional-managerial structure, paid out of surplus value and involving a degree of administration and control of the work process of others. At another level, these same head teachers often find themselves as glorified supply teachers filling in the gaps in hard pressed schools. They are therefore subject to contradictory pressures from above—to conform to the hierarchy which is such a dominant feature of the education system, to achieve results which improve the school's position in the education 'market'—and from below, to see their interests as much closer to the classroom teachers than to the managers of the local education authority.

Marx and the middle class

The growth of the middle class seems to contradict the basic ideas of Marx. From his earliest writings he assumed that the development of capitalism led to the creation of two contending classes and the eventual destruction of the various classes and social layers which existed outside of this polarisation.

The Communist Manifesto expressed this view:

> In the earlier epochs of history, we find almost everywhere a complicated arrangement of society into various orders, a manifold gradation of social rank. In ancient Rome we have patricians, knights, plebeians, slaves; in the Middle Ages, feudal lords, vassals, guild-masters, journeymen, apprentices, serfs; in almost all of these classes, again, subordinate gradations... The modern bourgeois society that has sprouted from the ruins of feudal society has not done away with class antagonisms. It has but established new classes, new conditions of oppression, new forms of struggle in place of the old ones.
>
> Our epoch, the epoch of the bourgeoisie, possesses, however, this distinctive feature: it has simplified the class antagonisms. Society as a whole is more and more splitting up into two great hostile camps, into two great classes directly facing each other: bourgeoisie and proletariat.[4]

The basic model described by Marx and Engels was essentially correct. The spread of capitalism meant the development of a powerful industrial class. The dynamic of the system, capital accumulation, led to the destruction of many of the old classes. The former ruling classes based on the old feudal order found their power and wealth superceded by the capitalist class; they declined as a serious social force in countries where capitalism developed most strongly and either faded from importance or—as in the case of Britain—became part of a capitalist ruling class. Some merchants who had flourished in the towns in the middle ages used their merchant capital to develop production in the mills and factories and so too became part of the emerging capitalist class, others were driven down into the working class.

The other classes which made up pre-capitalist societies also found themselves under intense pressure from both sides. Industrial production meant that within a relatively short period of time goods could be produced much more cheaply by machinery than by individuals in their workshops. Those such as artisans, craftsmen and journeymen became proletarianised, driven into the cities and forced to sell their labour power to the capitalists in order to live. For those who worked on the land the story was similar. Driven off the common land by enclosures and often not able to make a living for themselves, or finding their jobs on the farms also subject to mechanisation, they too were forced to become wage labourers.

Thus capitalist development was accompanied by the destruction of old classes as more and more people defined their position in terms of their relationship to capitalist exploitation. This has continued to be the case. Throughout the 20th century, therefore, there has been the development of monopoly capitalism on the one hand—societies dominated by fewer and fewer giant enterprises which tend to drive out or swallow up their competitors—and on the other hand the growth of a working class on a massive scale. In the newly industrialising countries this process is still at work: the old peasantry and small businessmen come under greater and greater pressure and therefore often end up as part of a growing proletariat in the face of capitalist expansion.

The development of the two major classes did not mean that all other classes completely disappeared. There were still small farmers and peasants, shopkeepers and publicans, doctors and lawyers, none of whom fitted into either of the main classes. This did not mean that they were totally outside the capitalist mode of production but rather that they were caught between the two contending classes.

The point was not that these classes ceased to exist but both that they tended to decline as a proportion of society as a whole, and that they could pursue no independent policy as a class separate from the two major classes.

So how does this square with the present situation, when the salaried 'middle classes' outlined above constitute around 15 to 20 percent of the population? They may be like the traditional petty bourgeoisie (small shopkeepers and businessmen) in terms of income and status, but there are crucial differences in other respects. The managerial and professional middle class is itself created by the capitalist system, and especially the scientific-technical revolution which has increasingly been a central feature of the 20th century. It is a middle class, therefore, which has arisen specifically from the production process. Whereas the 'old middle class' 'played no direct role in the capital accumulation process, whether on one side or the other' the 'new middle class' of salaried employees 'occupies its intermediate position not because it is *outside* the process of increasing capital, but because, as part of this process, it takes its characteristics from *both sides*.[5]

In addition, a typical member of the 'new middle class' does not tend to own any capital, but rather is a salaried employee. The vast majority are forced to sell their labour power on the market in order to live. It is this characteristic above all which leads to the idea that there is no fundamental division between the middle and working classes.

It is important when talking about definitions of the 'new middle class' (NMC) to understand that the term itself is misleading. It is not possible to talk about the NMC as a class, since it has no independence from either of the other classes, but takes it characteristics from both. Hal Draper puts it as follows:

> The petty bourgeois Janus faces two ways. On one side the petty bourgeois confront the capitalist, on the other side the worker. Two different lines of demarcation run through them: (1) If a line is drawn between property owners and the propertyless, then they are property owners; and as such they can rejoice in their identity with millionaires and thrill to orations on the Rights of Property. (2) If a line is drawn between those who live by their own labour and those who live by others' labour, then the petty bourgeois belong with the former, and they are workers; and as such they can appreciate the grievances of the working classes, including the proletariat.
>
> The petty bourgeoisie are therefore pulled in both directions. On the basis of the first demarcation, they can be taken in tow by the bourgeoisie. On the basis of the second, they have a community of interest, especially in the long run, with the proletariat as against the evils of the capitalist system.[6]

This characteristic of facing both ways leads to further difficulties in definition for socialists. There tend to be two distinct approaches among those on the left to the question of the middle class. Some answer the question, 'can the new middle classes be won to the side of the working class?' in the affirmative, and conclude that really the middle managers, professionals and so on are simply part of the proletariat—and an increasingly important part of the proletariat. By this view, everyone outside a tiny layer of top bosses and managers can be pulled into the definition of the working class.[7] It has the effect of blurring any distinction between the classes.

The second approach is to try to create a completely separate new middle class. The writer Nicos Poulantzas for example lumped together all non manual workers whether routine clerical or professional 'intellectuals' into the 'new petty bourgeoisie'.[8] Barbara and John Ehrenreich developed a theory of a 'professional managerial class' as a distinct class in an antagonistic relationship to the working class and which is specific to monopoly capitalism, consisting of 'salaried mental workers who do not own the means of production and whose major function in the social division of labour may be described broadly as the reproduction of capitalist culture and capitalist class relations.'[9]

The professional-managerial class's relation to the two major classes is that it is 'employed by capital *and* it manages, controls, has authority over labour'.[10] The problem with this definition of a separate class, which even the Ehrenreichs admit is fuzzy at both ends, is that it starts with a sociological definition. The Ehrenreichs see the development of a substantial professional class in the postwar US as evidenced by their education, their influence over ideas, their relative control over work, their consumption, without understanding that these characteristics are not static, nor are they features separate from capitalist social relations as a whole. As one critic of theirs argues:

> When people base class analysis on the concrete labour or specific attributes of types of jobs employed within the capitalist division of labour…the process whereby these forms of labour are produced, changed and reproduced anew, frequently under a new guise, completely eludes them.[11]

Capital is constantly acting in order to draw in new reserves of labour, to destroy old jobs and create new ones, to change the nature of certain sorts of work. To regard, for example, bank working or teaching as the same work as 100 years ago is to ignore the fundamental changes which have taken place in the jobs themselves and in their role under capitalism. Similarly with consumption. It is true that 'new middle class' lifestyles are often marked by conspicuous consumption: of designer clothes, several holidays a year, spending on households. But this cannot be seen simply as the distinctive behaviour of a class, rather it reflects the increased commodification of capitalist society which also has its impact on workers. Again, if we are talking about consistent patterns of consumption, then it is clear that at least some of the supposed 'new middle classes' have seen a cut back in consumption at all sorts of levels in recent years.

Both these attempts to define the 'new middle classes'—either that it is a 'new working class' and naturally allies itself with the proletariat, or that it is a separate professional-managerial class—fail for two reasons. Firstly they do not take into account the basic fact which Marx talked about when defining class: the relationship to the means of production and the production of surplus value. Instead they tend to judge class position by status, control and transmission of ideology—all of which may be important in trying to understand why particular groups of people act as they do, but cannot explain overall class relations. Secondly they do not understand the contradictory position in which many such people find themselves, and the likelihoods of these contradictions increasing inside a crisis ridden capitalism.

Contradictory situations

The trend towards the development of two major classes has not disappeared. So at the same time as there has been the growth of the various professional and managerial strata, a huge increase in the application of management techniques to all forms of the work process and so a concomitant growth of the number of managers, there has also been another pressure at work: towards the proletarianisation of a whole number of professional jobs. Workers in these jobs are being pushed further and further towards the working class. The process has been marked in clerical work for decades, as we saw above. Workers such as technicians and teachers also 'bear the mark of the proletarian condition'. How does this come about?

First, these [workers] become part of a mass labour market that assumes the characteristics of all labour markets, including the necessary existence of a reserve army of unemployed exercising a downward pressure on pay levels. And second, capital, as soon as it disposes of a mass of labour in any specialty…subjects that specialty to some of the forms of 'rationalisation' characteristic of the capitalist mode of production.[12]

This picture would be recognised only too well in every workplace—whether the banks or private industry with their downsizing, hospitals with the internal market putting more and more pressure on medical staff, schools with their increased emphasis on reports and tables or colleges which increasingly adopt education methods dominated by the market—bigger lectures, more 'throughput of students', longer hours and less holidays for lecturers.

Jobs which would have been perceived of as 'middle class' or professional a decade or two ago by many people who did them have been subject to major changes which make them much more like standard working class jobs. Take, for example, the case of journalism. For the large majority of journalists in magazine publishing and the provincial newspapers—and increasingly now on the national papers—computer technology has transformed the job. Journalists not only write their copy, they now have to sub edit it, often proof read it and make up the page. These would all be jobs once done by print workers of various descriptions. Journalists now find themselves tied to the computer which counts their key strokes and therefore is used to control the speed and intensity at which they work. Alongside the introduction of machinery, speed-up, intensification of work—all leading to the growth of the industrial injury RSI through too intense use of the keyboard—journalists' wages have taken a downward plunge overall.[13]

The process of rationalisation and market orientation in the former professions such as teaching and nursing now mean that even work which mostly involves dealing with human beings, and therefore by definition some of the most labour intensive and hardest to quantify, is subject to market pressures, such as viewing pupils as units in exam league tables or patients as beds to be cleared as rapidly as possible. Elements of individual care, the development of personal relationships through the work which were relatively important in distinguishing this work from work in factories or large impersonal offices, suffer increasingly under these pressures. We also see in the process the breakdown of the distinction between mental and manual labour which once characterised this sort of work.

The downward pressure on these groups of workers has led to dramatic changes in their composition and outlook over the past decades. There has been an increased tendency for teachers, nurses and the like to see themselves as workers; joining unions, taking industrial action and seeing their interests in common with other groups of organised workers, rather than in some way cut off from them. The first major strike action by teachers and town hall workers took place in the late 1960s and early 1970s. The political turmoil in teaching over recent years has been exacerbated by the direct attacks from government and media both ideologically and through spending cuts. Noticeably the response from the mass of teachers has been collective and organised, rather than individualistic—for example organising boycotts of school tests, supporting one day strikes against the cuts in particular areas and so on. The strength of such feeling is apparent in the militancy displayed at the teachers' union conferences, and the way in which even the more 'professional' and right wing unions have had to at least consider adopting militant action.[14] The lecturers' union, Natfhe, was involved in the largest dispute of 1994, accounting for 22 percent of all days 'lost' through strike action, because of the government and employers' attacks on lecturers' contracts.[15]

However, this has not simply been a one way development. At the same time that the mass of teachers, health workers, college lecturers, journalists or bank workers have found their wages and conditions pushed closer to the working class, a minority in those professions have found their career opportunities, salaries and lifestyles moving in the other direction. During the 1980s and early 1990s there has been the growth of a sizeable professional and managerial layer who are clearly and consciously being co-opted into helping to run the system. This is obvious when we look at the growth of management in, for example, the National Health Service, but it is a general phenomenon in every sector and industry and in all the advanced capitalist countries.

To take again one example: while the majority of lecturers in every sort of college in Britain have found their conditions worsen in recent years, a small minority have been pulled much more closely into administration and management of the college. This is to do with the introduction of the market into education, the need to maximise revenues from students, from hiring out college buildings for business or education seminars, for gaining business sponsorships or research grants. So while most lecturers in an FE college or in the new universities (former polytechnics) face shorter holidays, bigger classes and lectures, longer hours, the move to out of town sites, less job security and stagnant wages, those in the top grades and in management have become part of an elite layer with company cars, spacious offices and little contact with the everyday problems of teaching.

There is a process of differentiation therefore between the professionalisation of middle managers on the one hand and the pushing down of the conditions of the mass of the workforce on the other. We can see the contradictory situations facing the 'new middle class' if we take the extremes at both ends. Senior managers can find their way—and quite often do find their way—to being part of the capitalist class. Cedric Brown, the now retired and unlamented boss of British Gas, started as a middle manager in a publicly owned utility, rose in the management structure there and through privatisation was able to turn himself into an extremely wealthy member of the capitalist class, with share options, huge pension, personal driver and so on. At the other end of the scale, managers of high street branches of building societies have found themselves facing redundancy through successive waves of 'downsizing' and 'rationalisation' by their firms. They face long term unemployment, poverty and insecurity rather than any of the supposedly 'middle class' benefits they might have expected.[16]

It is clear that the pressures on these people are downwards towards the working class while the pull on the small number of senior executives will be towards open identification and—hopefully, from their point of view—incorporation into the capitalist class.

This does not mean that the 'new middle class' as a layer or series of layers in society will disappear. These are tendencies, not finished processes, and the capitalist class needs and will continue to need substantial layers of people to mediate between itself and the mass of exploited workers. This is true of the need for a complex structure of managers to ensure the smooth running of capitalist enterprises, the health, education and welfare system, and the state machine itself. It is also true of those who help

73

provide the ideological cement of society: the lawyers, professors, newspaper columnists, television administrators. Most of these people will still have a sufficient stake in the system to maintain their ideological commitment to it, however dissatisfied some individuals among them may be.

But the important thing is to see the middle layers as fluid, subject to contradictory pressures within capitalist society. It is more useful to see them like this than to accept the notion of 'contradictory class locations', which seems to suggest that the 'new middle class' takes certain characteristics from both of the major contending classes. This suggests a kind of hybrid class containing elements of both, rather than layers of people who face different pressures and who can be pulled in different directions depending on how great those pressures are or how close individuals are to either of the major classes.[17]

The political attitudes of the middle class reflect these contradictory pressures. Marx and Engels understood that the old petty bourgeoisie vacillated between the two contending classes and would be pulled in a particular direction depending on the balance of class forces. Engels wrote of the French middle classes during the 1848 revolution:

> The petty bourgeoisie play a mediating but very miserable role… They, and with them the Provisional Government, vacillate very much. The quieter everything gets, the more the government and the petty bourgeois party incline toward the big bourgeoisie; and the more disturbed things get, the more they side with the workers.[18]

Around the same time he described them as 'eternally tossed about between the hope of entering the ranks of the wealthier class, and the fear of being reduced to the state of proletarians or even paupers…this class is extremely vacillating in its views.'[19] Engels never changed his views, as he wrote to Marx's daughter Laura Lafargue in 1886:

> It will ever be the lot of the petty bourgeois—as a mass—to float undecidedly between the two great classes, one part to be crushed by the centralisation of capital, the other by the victory of the proletariat.[20]

The lack of independence as a class led to this political vacillation. Today it is just as prevalent, with sections of the 'new middle class' pushed towards quite deep hostility towards some of the worst aspects of capitalism—job insecurity, destruction of the environment, attacks on welfare—while at the same time fearing some of the more far reaching consequences of opposition to capitalism.

Trotsky writing about the threat of fascism in the 1920s and 1930s made a similar point, seeing the middle classes—who saw all of their old certainties destroyed by the crisis in inter-war Europe—as having the potential to be pulled towards socialist politics or equally to be pulled towards reactionary, fascist politics. The key, he argued, was that they would follow whichever class was the more decisive. If the capitalist class used its power to attack workers and so solve its problems through worsening their conditions, then it could win sections of the middle class to its support. If, on the other hand, the workers' movement could show that it had a solution to the problems of humanity, then it would be able to give a political lead to the middle layers of society. After all, the mass of these people had a similar interest alongside the working class in ending inflation, unemployment and the squeezing of their living standards.[21]

But this identification was not—and is not—automatic. The situation of many of the middle classes means that they have some hopes of an individual way out of the crisis—however illusory such hopes may be. Prospects of promotion, of owning a small business, of dropping out of the 'rat race' and moving to the country, all have an appeal to such people. In addition, their attitudes will tend to reinforce more reactionary or individualistic views. At the most basic level, they are much more likely to vote Tory.[22] Support for incomes policies to help the low paid drops from around 80 percent among both manual workers and low grade white collar workers to 60 percent among the 'salariat'. Around 45 percent of professionals, managers and employers supported redistribution of income and wealth to 'ordinary working people' in another study, while 65-70 percent of lower grades—both manual and non manual—did.[23] Those who believe social services and benefits are extremely important differ markedly by class.[24] A survey which considered people's attitudes to individual rights, showed that middle class people are more liberal on issues such as right to privacy. But interestingly on two key issues—the right to be rehoused if homeless and the right to silence in court—working class opinion is much more liberal.[25]

Many such people can be pushed further towards collective solutions and left wing politics by the impact of the crisis, which promises greater misery for the vast majority while a tiny minority benefit. But this is only possible if we develop an analysis which does not confuse the capitalist class with the middle class or the middle class with the working class, and which understands the contradictory situations in which the middle classes find themselves.

A class for itself

Perhaps the greatest difficulty in discussing class comes when we try to make the link between what constitutes a class objectively and how that class develops revolutionary ideas and becomes capable of making a revolution. The leap that this necessitates between the working class as it is and what it has to become in order to make such a revolution is so immense that it seems impossible to bridge. Workers are atomised and divided. Each worker lives within his or her family, separated off from wider society for much of the time. Workers are divided along lines of race, sex, nation, between manual and white collar work. They are split between different workplaces, varying immensely in terms of size, work process and organisation. Politically, although Labour is the dominant party among workers, significant numbers of both white collar and manual workers vote Tory. And there are millions of people in Britain today whose consciousness of their class position does not correspond to their actual position.

How do workers begin to cut through these confusions and so come together as a class? After all, if the working class is so big and so powerful, how is it that we seem as far away from a socialist society as ever? And if the working class is so revolutionary then why does it not make a revolution?

Workers' position in capitalist society

Throughout the previous chapters we have talked about the major differences between the classes in terms of income, attitudes and expectations. These inequalities are a direct result of workers' relationship to the means of production—the fact that they are exploited. But this economic relationship pervades the whole of their lives. It means that the ideas which confront workers—ideas which they receive through the education system, through the media, through the general 'common sense' which dominates society—basically accept the status quo. It is assumed that our rulers have the right to rule, that nothing can be achieved except through gradual change, that everyone is equal before the law. In one of their most famous passages Marx and Engels wrote:

> The ideas of the ruling class are in every epoch the ruling ideas: ie, the class, which is the ruling *material* force of society, is at the same time its ruling *intellectual* force. The class which has the means of material production at its disposal, has control at the same time over the means of mental production.[1]

Not only do the employers own the factories and offices, they also ensure to the best of their abilities that their ideas remain the ruling ideas. The whole structure of society—the education system, the family, the state machine, the media—is designed so that these ideas are transmitted as though they were the most natural thing in the world. So we are constantly faced with beliefs which defend the right of our rulers to rule. We are told that bosses deserve their incomes and lifestyles because they take risks and work harder, that we all have a 'national interest' which binds us together, that any attempt to fundamentally change society has been doomed to failure.

Capitalist exploitation also creates the alienation of workers. Workers produce the wealth in society, but are cut off from the products of their labour. These products appear as estranged from any control that workers might have over them. Workers feel a sense of powerlessness not just at work but in every aspect of their lives.

> For the proletarians...the condition of their existence, labour, and with it all the conditions of existence governing modern society, have become something accidental, something over

which they, as separate individuals, have no control, and over which no *social* organisation can give them control.[2]

In addition, the things which workers produce confront them as commodities, goods to be bought and sold in the market. Commodities are a product of social relations—of the exploitation of workers—but appear as objects which determine social relations. They seem to workers as something detached from their work and their life, which can only be obtained by resort to the market. Everything has a price including both what they produce and their own labour power.

It is no wonder that workers, deprived of the means of production and separated from the products of their labour, see work not as the most meaningful part of life but as a sacrifice of their life. The idyllic properties invested in the idea of retirement from work, or even the arrival of the weekend or Friday night, within popular mythology, demonstrate how much work is seen as an unpleasant reality which has to be got through in order to begin 'living'. Yet the estrangement and lack of control that workers feel about the world around them ensure that leisure too is dominated by alienation—there is no escape from the market and from the world of commodities.

It is precisely this condition which leads workers to see themselves other than as workers. It is very common today for workers to be seen simply as consumers. Many argue that the collective identity nurtured by large factories, company towns or big working class estates, leisure time dominated by mass activities such as attending football matches or day trips to Blackpool, has disappeared. Now individuals go to work separately in cars, work in smaller units, live in Brookside-like housing developments and watch videos. They identify themselves not by class position but by what they spend, how they spend it and how they dress.

Increasingly since the 1950s, the labour market has ceased to be a primary source of identity. It has yielded its dominant position to the consumer market. People are, it is said, no longer what they do, but what they have, what they own. Perhaps this is why, when we look at a crowd of people, it no longer makes sense to ask whether they are working class or middle class. All we see is a collection of individuals going about their chosen business, freed from the limitations that bound earlier generations to their place in society.[3]

There are of course very important partial truths in such statements. The attitude of most individuals is to define themselves in terms of their personal relationships, their hobbies and other such factors. This is not, of course, a new phenomenon. Throughout the 20th century, working class cultural habits, fashion and holidays have all played a significant part in workers' lives.

But the consumerism and individuality exist precisely because of the life experience of workers. When you have no control over the working day, and little control over where you work, how you do your work and what satisfaction you get from the job, it is hardly surprising that everything outside work is invested with great importance. When individuality is denied to workers over all the important decisions in their lives, then the importance of being able to wear designer clothes (or at least cheap copies), decorate your house slightly differently from your neighbours or go on foreign holidays becomes much greater. When workers' lives are routine, humdrum and often downright unpleasant at work, then to have a home and family—and especially to have children who will be able to lead better lives than you have done—becomes the centre of life.

The problem of course is that all these 'escapes' from the world of work are really no escape. They provide some relief and happiness—and certainly people who are denied even these basics inside capitalist society usually feel much worse off without them—but they cannot provide an alternative to the market and the system of exploitation.

> The social structure, built upon the market, is such that relations between individuals and social groups do not take place directly, as cooperative human encounters, but through the market as relations of purchase and sale. Thus the more social life becomes a dense and close network of interlocked activities in which people are totally interdependent, the more atomised they become and the more their contacts with one another separate them instead of bringing them closer.[4]

So precisely the aspects of life which seem to offer most relief in fact do the opposite. Even in areas where workers might try to express their individual talents or interests in a different way, the market acts in order to embrace them and in the process robs them of anything 'individual' or 'different':

So enterprising is capital that even where the effort is made by one or another section of the population to find a way to nature, sport, or art through personal activity and amateur or 'underground' innovation, these activities are rapidly incorporated into the market so far as possible.[5]

For workers to define themselves as consumers therefore is far from being an escape from alienation—it is an affirmation of their alienation, and an affirmation that in a world based on commodity production 'the source of status is no longer the ability to make many things but simply the ability to purchase them'.[6] That ability to purchase commodities may be central to workers' lives, especially since those such as the unemployed or pensioners who are effectively without such ability are at the bottom of the pile within capitalist society, but its importance diminishes the more workers begin to see themselves as part of a collective. The more they act to overcome the atomisation of their lives—and this means involvement in collective struggle—the more the same people who once placed such store by clothes or cars begin to see such collective action as more important.

It would seem from the above that the situation of workers makes it extremely difficult for them to overcome their subordinate role as a class, let alone be able to organise a new sort of society. The working class is very different, for example, from the emergent capitalist class—the bourgeoisie—which overthrew the old feudal economies in countries such as England and France and were able to establish modern capitalist states. The bourgeoisie was able to develop itself as a minority class within the old feudal society. It developed its own strongholds in the towns, its own industries, its own schools and universities, even its own religion. It was able therefore to build its wealth and power which allowed it then to make the revolution and establish its rule.

The working class today is not able to develop similar sorts of class institutions of its own inside capitalist society. It owns no property and has no power except its ability to produce the wealth of society. It is only by realising this power—by taking control of the means of production and by destroying the old capitalist state—that it is capable of making its own socialist revolution. This can only be done collectively, because the working class produces and works collectively. It is only in the process of doing so that it will be able to overcome its atomisation and alienation and become a fully conscious class:

> Both for the production on a mass scale of this communist consciousness, and for the success of the cause itself, the alteration of men on a mass scale is necessary, an alteration which can only take place in a practical movement, a *revolution*; this revolution is necessary, therefore, not only because the *ruling* class cannot be overthrown in any other way, but also because the class *overthrowing* it can only in a revolution succeed in ridding itself of all the muck of ages and become fitted to found society anew.[7]

It was this that Marx talked about when he made a distinction between the working class as a class in itself and a working class *for itself*.[8] He meant by this that the working class existed as a class in objective terms but had to learn how to struggle and develop its own ideas in order to move towards class consciousness. It was only when the struggle and ideas had reached such a level that workers' revolution became possible that the working class could become a fully conscious class.

Of course there is a huge leap from one to the other—most workers do not go straight from accepting much of the system to suddenly completely opposing it. Instead the day to day battles of workers all become lessons in the school of class struggle and help them to develop their ideas and activity to a higher level. Marx wrote about the connection between economic and political fights:

> The attempt in a particular factory or even in a trade to force a shorter working week out of individual capitalists by strikes, etc, is a purely economic movement. On the other hand the movement to force through an eight hour *law* is a *political* movement. And in this way, out of the separate economic movements of the workers there grows up everywhere a *political* movement, that is to say, a movement of the *class*, with the object of enforcing its interests in a general form, in the form of possessing general, socially coercive force. While these movements presuppose a certain degree of previous organisation, they are equally a means of developing this organisation.[9]

The key point here is that workers change and develop their ideas in struggle. As Hal Draper has written: 'The working class is *atomised* when it is unorganised. Class organisation brings class characteristics to the fore, and, as a function of organisation, class characteristics increasingly take precedence over merely individual reactions, the greater the scale of class involvement.'[10]

Organisation comes from struggle. The class struggle is a daily feature of life coming from the daily experience of workers. Speed-up at work, cuts in welfare, worsening public transport and higher taxes are all demonstrations of the class struggle—the way in which the ruling class attempts to extract an even greater share of the surplus produced at the expense of workers. This experience tends to give many workers at least some sense of being workers and of suffering exploitation. But their perception that there is something wrong with the system, that they are being made to work too hard, or that all their wages seem to go as soon as they receive them, is often coupled with a sense of powerlessness to do anything.

Trade union organisation is a reflection of this combined set of ideas. It is a perception that much is wrong with the world and that working people are on the receiving end of it, alongside the feeling that nothing fundamental can ever change.

Unionisation and struggle

Unions are themselves products of workers' struggle. They have rarely been set up without opposition from the employers and their hangers on. In Britain, their origins go back nearly 200 years, when unions were formed illegally against a background of repression and brutality as the Industrial Revolution swept everything before it. Those who organised the unions (or swore illegal oaths, as the law put it) were subject to imprisonment, harassment and even transportation. Yet persistently the new working class joined trade unions. The first organised movement of the working class around Chartism gave the impetus to trade unionism, with the first general strike in the textile districts and elsewhere in 1842.

Time and again workers who have been regarded as lacking in militancy, inexperienced, even unorganisable, have organised together to defend themselves from the employers' attacks. In Britain today the decline of old and traditionally well organised groups of workers, for example the miners and the dockers, has not meant the end to union organisation. Instead new groups of workers have developed militancy and traditions—postal workers, civil servants, bank workers, shop workers are now highly likely to be in unions and many will have experienced at least some strike action. The change in the past two decades, with the growth of these new sectors of organisation and the steep decline of some traditional industries, has led to some dramatic changes in perception. Today, for example, most people familiar with the organised working class movement would recognise postal workers as one of the most militant and powerful groups of workers, who have built their organisation through a series of battles with post office management. Printers have, however, seen a decline in their traditionally strong unions. Yet in the early 1970s everyone would have taken for granted the exact opposite: printers were among the strongest organised workers, while post office workers suffered a major defeat in their national strike in 1971 and were considered much weaker.

The same has been true in the past. The explosion of 'new unionism' in the late 1880s centred in the East End of London—regarded at the time as one gigantic 'underclass'. Its motor force was unskilled workers—dockers, seasonal gas workers, the 'match girls'—and large components of the most militant trade unionists were women and Irish immigrants. Will Thorne wrote of the founding of the gas workers' union in 1889: 'The idea caught on; enthusiasm was at a high pitch, and within two weeks we had over 3,000 men in the union. Never before had men responded like they did. For months London was ablaze.'[11]

The strikes won union organisation and established the basis of what were to become the big general unions inside British industry. The later upheavals in British working class history had a similar effect. The Great Unrest between 1910 and 1914 led to the strengthening of groups such as the railway workers and the miners, who found themselves in conflict with both the employers and the state. Again in the 1930s there was a struggle inside the new industries to win workers' rights and unionisation. These new industries were dominated by workers with no political traditions—women workers who might previously have been in domestic service or former agricultural workers who could no longer get a living in the rural areas. They lacked any knowledge and tradition of organising. Those who came from the traditionally well organised areas—especially unemployed miners who went to work in Coventry or Oxford—at first found themselves very isolated in their attempts to build unions or politicise the workforce. But in the course of the 1930s many of these same workers were transformed into workplace militants. Here is the description of one factory in Oxford, Pressed Steel, in 1938 when the union branch secretary was sacked:

> The workers marched right through the factory from one end to the other... They had a meeting in the Press Shop and there were workers everywhere—stenographers, typists, God knows what, all over the machines taking the stuff down that the workers who were the leaders, who were on the top of the presses, were saying. And they turned machines over, they turned car bodies over. Just erupted.[12]

So new, inexperienced and weak groups of workers became militant, strong and experienced in the course of struggle. It is important to stress this today when it is a common argument that, 'we're not a strong group of workers like the dockers', or that, 'where I work we don't have the power that coal miners do.' The power of the working class is not an absolute question. It too is something which is formed and developed in the course of workers taking action. So the strike by workers at Dunne's stores in Ireland which included large numbers of part time and women workers and which ended in victory, demonstrated how a traditionally weak group of workers could develop their power. The impact of this strike on the trade union movement in Ireland has been dramatic:

> The biggest single increase in membership of any union last year [1995] was Mandate, which recruited 2,088 new members, of whom 1,508 were women. This was largely as a result of the strike at Dunne's stores. This year could tell a similar story. The membership of the Irish Nurses' Organisation has grown by almost 3,000 during the last couple of months of industrial unrest. Again the overwhelming majority of recruits are women.[13]

At the same time, groups of workers traditionally seen as strong can fail to use their potential power and so be defeated. There was a catalogue of such disputes in the 1980s including the steel workers' strike in 1980, the print workers at Wapping in 1986 and the failed campaign to prevent pit closures which the NUM followed in 1992-3. How workers fight and whether they fight helps to determine how strong and powerful they then become, and the consciousness which develops from fresh struggles.

Of course it is true that some groups of workers have more obvious and direct power than others. If print workers strike for a few hours, they can cost their employers huge sums in lost revenue and advertising. Electrical power workers are potentially able to paralyse the whole of industry by the action of a very small number of workers. But it is also the case that bank workers can have a rapid and damaging effect on their employers' profits, as can workers in Sainsbury's. Even workers who are not directly making profits for a particular capitalist have more economic and social power than our rulers would have us believe. For example, teachers and health workers, who contribute indirectly to the production of surplus value, can have a financial effect, even if it is not felt so rapidly. The ruling class in general fears nearly any withdrawal of labour, not just for financial reasons but because of the threat to social stability. It is too damaging for the ruling class to allow a strike among, for example, workers in unemployment benefit offices, for fear of the social upheaval that this would create.

The generally low level of struggle in Britain in recent years reinforces the dominant view that workers lack power. But it is obvious that those workers who have engaged in even partial struggles have begun to develop a power which would not have been thought possible at one time. Teachers' and nurses' action has forced their work conditions and their union activities to the very centre of political debate and developed a level of militancy and consciousness quite different from any that had previously existed in those industries.

However there are necessarily limits to how far this change of consciousness goes. Partly this is because of the nature of trade union struggle itself. It was described by the German revolutionary Rosa Luxemburg as a 'labour of Sisyphus'. Sisyphus was a figure in Greek mythology forever destined to push a stone up a hill only for it to roll down again as soon as he got near the top, thus forcing him to start again. Because trade union struggle is essentially defensive under capitalism the same process occurs— workers make advances, but because they never succeed in overthrowing the system by this method, they find the gains they have made constantly under attack by the employers.

The role of the trade union leaders fits this process. They see themselves as essentially balancing between capital and labour—

wanting to ameliorate the conditions of their members but at the same time fearful that any struggle which goes 'too far' will begin to threaten the whole foundations of capitalist society. The trade union leaders prefer periods of capitalist expansion, when their demands for slightly higher wages, or a shorter working day, are compatible with what the system seems able to give. In periods of crisis they become disoriented, realising that such demands can in some situations threaten the whole future of capitalism itself, and realising equally that they cannot deliver the reforms which their members require and for which they increasingly clamour.

It is this which explains the vacillations of the union leaders between confronting the system and compromising with it. Many trade union members accept this compromise as the best they can get out of a system over which they have no direct control. So struggle changes consciousness, but not always to an understanding of the need for a revolutionary overthrow of society.

The unevenness inside the working class is the product of capitalism itself. Workers are divided in every conceivable way and are led to believe themselves different from one another. Their experiences are also very different, depending on what jobs they do, what sort of workplace they are in, what their background is. Much of this unevenness is overcome in struggle, but by no means all of it. That is why a workers' party is needed.

Party and class

The working class has to have a party to overcome the contradiction between its potential revolutionary role and its actual situation. To overcome this contradiction requires a conscious struggle by an organised minority which aims both to win much larger numbers directly to its ranks, but also to give a lead to other workers who may still be at least partly influenced by the union leaders or the Labour Party. Any revolutionary party has to avoid the dangers of workers' organisation which has historically dogged the movement: that it either substitutes for the working class movement or that it assumes its interests and those of the whole working class are identical. The first danger can be summed up by those organisations who believe it is enough simply to proclaim themselves the 'workers' party' for them to become it, and who think that adoption of the 'correct' programme will eventually lead the working class (or at least its 'vanguard') to their banner. Most of such organisations have found themselves incapable of moving beyond the size and status of a sect, and far from their politics being proved correct when the struggle rises, have found themselves on the sidelines when workers do move.

The second sort of party—which represents the whole working class—is most usually the Labour Party model. This sort of party ignores questions of struggle and consciousness as having much to do with its organisation, is most concerned with taking over the existing social institutions and running them on behalf of workers, and therefore takes its politics from the lowest common denominator. Workers' ideas are taken as given—in this view, there will always be racists and sexists inside the working class movement, so all points of view have to be encompassed if all workers are to be represented within the party. In reality, this disarms the most class conscious and revolutionary workers within such a party and leads to an organisation whose structures and organisation are characterised by opportunism and compromise.

A genuine revolutionary party has to break quite sharply from both such models. It has to be rooted in the working class movement, with organic links to the most advanced sections of the working class. Partly this means that the revolutionary party has to be the *memory* of the working class movement. Franz Jakubowski writes:

> While the class as a whole recognises its tasks only in the course of struggle, a part of it, the party, already knows the direction from the experience of previous struggles.[14]

The party's role is partly arguing and discussing inside the working class movement, getting across the tradition of the movement, the lessons of past defeats and the theoretical ideas which have developed from the movement. However, the party has to learn from the class—because the working class movement is itself constantly developing, throwing up new forms of organisation and struggle, looking to new ways out of the crisis. In this sense, the party can often be not in advance of the class, but lagging behind its most class conscious elements. The experience of outbreaks of revolution or even of mass strikes, where once passive workers move swiftly into action, and revolutionary socialists are taken by surprise by their actions, proves this only too well. Then millions of workers can look towards the revolutionary overthrow of the system, because they see that the path of reform is closed. In such situations they set up their own forms of organisation and begin to run society themselves. The establishment of workers' councils is a feature of workers' revolutions as they try to establish workers' power. This is why Lenin could write during the 1905 Russian revolution that the working class is instinctively social democratic (by which he meant revolutionary).

Perhaps this relationship between the party and the class can be summed up as: 'The party is simultaneously the *product* and the *producer* of class consciousness'.[15]

So the party is rooted in the day to day struggles of workers and at the same time attempts to generalise and develop its ideas out of these struggles. Only a party where there is a constant interaction between the two can be capable of giving a lead to workers' struggles as they develop, and help to take them beyond limited defensive struggles to a more general onslaught against capitalism. And only in the process of this happening can workers themselves begin to come to consciousness and begin to see themselves not simply as the object of history who sells his or her labour power as a commodity, but capable of acting in order to change history.

Because class is a living relationship to the means of production, it is precisely in the course of such struggles that workers come together as a class—when all the individualism, the differences, the separations begin to be overcome and workers see their collective strength and their own power.

Modern capitalism has created a bigger and bigger working class, has spread the market to every area of life and to every part of the world, has deepened the crisis so that more and more workers are forced to struggle and so begin to develop a sense of this power. The major battles which lie ahead, as the ruling classes internationally attempt to cut into workers' living standards in order to preserve their profits, will make greater numbers of workers conscious of the need to fight the system—and aware of their role as a class which has the potential to make a revolution.

Notes

1 What is class?

1   *The Social Context of British Politics,* David Coates (London 1984) p101-103
2   *Social Trends 24,* HMSO (London 1994), p117
3   *Financial Times,* London,25-26 February, 1995
4   *Social Trends 24,* HMSO (London 1994), p85
5   *Social Trends 21,* HMSO (London 1991), p180
6   *Social Trends 25,* HMSO (London 1995), p220-221
7   The General Household Survey quoted in *Social Trends 21,* HMSO (London 1991), p96
8   *Social Trends 21,* HMSO (London 1991), p95. These figures exclude pension fund holdings and the value of houses.
9   See *Class in a Capitalist Society,* John Westergaard and Henrietta Resler (London 1975), p41
10 Ibid, p114
11 Ibid, p299
12 *Two Nations? The Inheritance of Poverty and Affluence,* Paul Johnson and Howard Reed, The Institute for Fiscal Studies (London 1996), p10
13 *The Observer,* London, 14 April 1996
14 *Social Trends 24,* HMSO (London 1994), p172
15 *The Age of Extremes,* Eric Hobsbawm (London 1994), p307
16 A total of 1.7 million new car registrations were recorded in 1992, for example, out of a total of 22.3 million cars and light vans on the road. *Social Trends 24,* HMSO (London 1994), p171
17 *The Communist Manifesto (*Tirana 1981), p26
18 *The German Ideology,* Karl Marx and Frederick Engels (London 1965), p45
19 *The Communist Manifesto,* op cit, p27
20 Ibid, p39
21 *The Class Struggle in the Ancient Greek World,* GEM de Ste Croix (London 1981) p43
22 *The Holy Family* in *Collected Works vol IV,* Karl Marx and Frederick Engels (London), p37
23 *The Making of the English Working Class,* EP Thompson, (London 1968), p8-9
24 *The Poverty of Philosophy* in *Collected Works vol VI,* Karl Marx, p210-11
25 A common view among those historians and writers connected to the former Communist Party. See Eric Hobsbawm, *The Forward*

     March of Labour Halted, Ed Martin Jacques and Francis
     Mulhern (London 1981)
26   *Capital vol III*, Karl Marx, (London 1974), p885

2 'The most revolutionary class'

1   *Talking Work: An Oral History,* Trevor Blackwell and Jeremy
     Seabrook (London 1996) p208
2   I am grateful to Alex Callinicos for this point
3   *Talking Work*, op cit, p150
4   *The Age of Extremes*, Eric Hobsbawm (London 1994), p303
5   *Industry and Empire*, Eric Hobsbawm (London 1969), p110
6   Ibid, p109
7   Ibid, p116
8   *Capitalism, Culture and Decline in Britain,* WD Rubinstein,
     (London 1993), p32
9   See *Industry and Empire,* p154 which quotes a survey which puts
     the 'manual labour class' at 77 percent of the population.
10   Ibid p195
11   See 'Women's work in 19th century London', Sally Alexander, in
     The Rights and Wrongs of Women, Ed Juliet Mitchell and Ann
     Oakley (London 1976), p59-111
12   *Britain in the 1930s*, Noreen Branson and Margot Heinemann,
     (London 1973), p126-129
13   *Industry and Empire,* op cit, p218
14   *Labour and Monopoly Capital*, Harry Braverman (London 1974),
     p239
15   *Capitalism, Culture and Decline in Britain*, WD Rubinstein, p33
16   *Labour Market Trends (*London March 1996), p111
17   *The Age of Extremes*, op cit, p304
18   *Labour and Monopoly Capital*, op cit, p360
19   'The Family wage' Michele Barrett and Mary McIntosh in *The
     Changing Experience of Women*, Ed Whitelegg (Oxford 1982), p74
20   Quoted in *Wives and Mothers in Victorian Industry*, Margaret
     Hewitt (London 1958), p63-4
21   *Labour Market Trends (*London March 1996), p111
22   *The Dynamics of Workplace Unionism*, Ralph Darlington,
     (London 1994), p8
23   *Labour Market Trends (*London March 1996), p110
24   *Social Trends 26 (*London 1996), p88
25   Ibid, p90
26   Ibid, p90
27   Survey by Business Strategies, quoted in the *Financial Times,*
     London, 8 March 1996 p11
28   *Financial Times,* ibid
29   *Financial Times,* ibid
30   *Social Trends 25* (London 1995), p76

31 Ibid, p68
32 *The Economist,* London, 5 March, 1994
33 Figures quoted in *Sex Class and Socialism,* Lindsey German, (London 1994), p106
34 *Social Trends 25,* op cit, p69
35 Ibid, p69
36 *About Time,* Patricia Hewitt (London 1993), p15
37 *Labour Market Trends,* March 1996, op cit, p97
38 *Flexible labour? Employment and training in new service industries,* Kevin Doogan (University of Bristol 1992), p23
39 For details on this see Women and Employment: a lifetime perspective, J Martin and C Roberts, HMSO (London 1984)
40 *The Genesis of Modern Management,* Sidney Pollard (Cambridge Mass 1965), p137-9, 153-5 quoted in *Labour and Monopoly Capital,* Harry Braverman (London 1974), p260
41 Braverman, ibid, p295
42 Braverman, ibid, p297
43 *Social Trends 25,* op cit, p86-87
44 Labour Market Trends, March 1996, op cit, p546
45 *Social Trends 25,* op cit, p74
46 Ibid, p74
47 *Talking Work*: *An Oral History,* Trevor Blackwell and Jeremy Seabrook (London 1996), p29
48 *Labour's Turning Point,* Eric Hobsbawm (Brighton 1974) xvii-xviii
49 *Capital vol I,* Karl Marx (London 1974), p393-99
50 *Talking Work,* op cit, p94
51 See for example *The First Shop Stewards Movement,* James Hinton (London 1973), and *Labour's Turning Point,* Hobsbawm, op cit
52 Quoted in *The Dynamics of Workplace Unionism,* Ralph Darlington (London 1994), p139
53 Households Below Average Income 1979-1992, HMSO (London 1995), p20
54 *Class: Where Do You Stand?* Greg Hadfield and Mark Skipworth (London 1994), p88-89
55 *Social Trends 25,* op cit, p151
56 See *The Culture of Contentment,* J K Galbraith (London 1992)
57 Christopher Huhne 'Tory Choice that hits the Poorest' *Independent on Sunday,* London, 4 July 1993
58 Quoted in *The 'Underclass' Debate,* Michael Katz (Oxford 1993), p7
59 *Who Gets What?,* John Westergaard (Cambridge 1995), p116-117
60 *The Culture of Contentment,* op cit, p31
61 Low Pay Unit estimates taken from *Out of poverty towards prosperity,* NUCPS and Low Pay Unit (London 1995), p8
62 Ibid, p14
63 *Capital vol I,* Karl Marx (London 1974), pp 589-606
64 Figures quoted in 'Engels and the Condition of the Working Class

today', Doria Pilling, in *The Condition of Britain*, Eds John Lea and Geoff Pilling (London 1996), p19

65 *The Guardian*, London, 28 May 1996
66 *The Financial Times*, London, 17 April 1996
67 *Social Trends 24* (London 1994), p63-4
68 *The Condition of Britain*, Doria Pilling, op cit, p32
69 'The facts of life on a low income', Catherine Pepinster, *Independent on Sunday*, London, 2 June 1996
70 *Social Trends 24* (London 1994), p110
71 Quoted in *Who Gets What*, Westergaard, op cit, p149
72 'She is, are you?', Dave Hill, *Observer Life* magazine, London, 31 March 1996 p26

3 Born to rule

1 *Class in a Capitalist Society*, John Westergaard and Henrietta Resler (London 1975), p346
2 *Who Gets What?*, John Westergaard (Cambridge 1995), p127-128
3 *The Communist Manifesto*, Karl Marx and Frederick Engels (Tirana, 1981), p26
4 *Labour and Monopoly Capital*, Harry Braverman (London 1974), p258-9
5 *Class in a Capitalist Society*, op cit, p53
6 *Labour and Monopoly Capital*, op cit, p405
7 *Class: Where Do You Stand?*, Greg Hadfield and Mark Skipworth (London 1994), p73-74
8 For example, the US government in the late 19th century was forced to use its state power directly to impose order on the 'wild west' and to resolve the conflicts between different local capitals
9 *Anti Dühring* in *Collected Works vol 25*, Karl Marx and Frederick Engels (Moscow 1987), p266
10 *Class in a Capitalist Society*, op cit, p276
11 *Capital vol III*, Karl Marx (London 1974), p197
12 Ibid, p253
13 *Business Age 500*, Number 47 (London 1994), p24
14 *Class and Capitalist Society*, Westergaard and Resler, p114
15 Ibid, p376
16 Ibid, p376. See for example Veuve Cliquot champagne advert *The Independent*, London, 21 May 1996
17 *Ideology and Superstructure in Historical Materialism*, Franz Jakubowski (London 1990), p110
18 Ibid, p110

4 Caught in the middle?

1 Tony Parsons 'A middle class hero is something to be', *Daily Mirror*, London, 15 April, 1996, p7

2   'Class conflict; the human dimension', Sandy Carter in *Between Labour and Capital*, Ed Pat Walker (Brighton 1979), p101

3   *Labour and Monopoly Capital*, Harry Braverman (London 1974), p405

4   *The Communist Manifesto* (Tirana 1981), p27

5   *Labour and Monopoly Capital*, Braverman , op cit, p407

6   *Karl Marx's Theory of Revolution*, Hal Draper (New York 1978), p292

7   This was a more current view in the late 1960s and early 1970s. It tended to be an explanation for the failure of traditional manual workers to act politically (for example in the US in the late 1960s) whereas the college educated professionals tended to have more radical views.

8   'On social classes', Nicos Poulantzas in *New Left Review* (London), no 78 March April, 1973

9   'The professional-managerial class', Barbara and John Ehrenreich in *Between Labour and Capital*, op cit, p12

10 Ibid, p18

11 'Between the lines' Robert Shaeffer and James Weinstein in *Between Labour and Capital*, ibid, p149

12 *Labour and Monopoly Capital*, op cit, p407-8

13 For example the wages of female journalists, authors and writers in 1993 stood at £366.5 gross, with 10 percent receiving less than £221.5 a week gross and 38 percent earning less than £300 before tax. *New Earnings Survey 1993*, Part A, HMSO (London), pA9.3

14 The NASUWT union, largest apart from the traditionally most militant NUT, and the ATL, the most 'professional' teachers' union, have in recent years been forced to at least talk about taking action.

15 *Employment Gazette*, London, July 1995, p281

16 *Independent on Sunday*, London, 28 April, 1996

17 The formulation put by Erik Olin Wright that the middle classes occupy 'contradictory class locations' seems to me a rather rigid and formulaic way of looking at the question and doesn't take into account this fluidity. He also tends to see the position of the middle classes stemming from control rather than from their relation to the extraction of surplus value. So he writes: 'intellectuals typically occupy a contradictory class location between the working class and the petty bourgeoisie at the economic level, but between the working class and the bourgeoisie at the ideological level.' What is this supposed to mean, apart from a complete separation between the ideological and the economic spheres which leads to a conception of class which is more about filling particular 'spaces' for individuals than about understanding class as a dynamic relationship. 'Intellectuals and the Class Structure of Capitalist Society', Erik Olin Wright in *Between Labour and Capital* (Brighton 1979),

p204. I am grateful to Jon Gubbay for a critical view of Wright in 'A Defence of Marxist Class Analysis—and a critique of Wright's Neo-Weberian Synthesis'and to Alex Callinicos who discusses Wright in *The Changing Working Class* (London), p27-36

18 Frederick Engels' letter to Emil Blank quoted in *Karl Marx's Theory of Revolution vol II*, Draper, op cit, p296

19 Ibid, p298

20 Ibid, p304

21 *Fascism, Stalinism and the United Front*, Leon Trotsky (London 1989), p41-43

22 See *The British Electorate 1963-1992*, Ivor Crewe, Anthony Fox and Neil Day (Cambridge 1995), p19

23 Studies quoted in *Who Gets What?*, John Westergaard (Cambridge 1995), p173-4

24 *The British Electorate*, op cit, p372

25 Poll reported in the *Independent*, London, 30 May 1995, p13

5 A class for itself

1   *The German Ideology,* Karl Marx and Frederick Engels (London 1965), p60

2   Ibid, p94

3   *Talking Work*, Trevor Blackwell and Jeremy Seabrook (London 1996), p200

4   *Labour and Monopoly Capital*, Harry Braverman (London 1974), p277

5   Ibid, p279

6   Ibid, p276

7   *The German Ideology,* op cit, p86

8   *The Poverty of Philosophy* in *Collected Works vol VI*, Karl Marx, p210-211

9   *Marx and Engels Selected Works vol 2*, 23 November 1871, p423 quoted in Chris Bambery, 'Marx and the Unions' in *International Socialism 26 (*London Spring 1985), p83

10 *Karl Marx's Theory of Revolution vol II*, Hal Draper (New York 1978), p40

11 *Labour's Turning Point,* Eric Hobsbawm (Brighton 1974), p80

12 *The British Communist Party and the Trade Unions*, Nina Fishman (London 1994), p217

13 'Trade unions in Republic gained nearly 10,000 members last year' by Padraig Yeates, *Irish Times,* Dublin 28 May 1996

14 *Ideology and Superstructure in Historical Materialism*, Franz Jakubowski (London 1990), p123

15 Ibid, p123